AS IF

**If we live by the Spirit,
we should also walk by the Spirit**

GRAEME SCHULTZ

Gobsmacked Publishing

All Scripture quotations, unless otherwise indicated, are taken from the Holy Bible, New International Version®, NIV®. Copyright ©1973, 1978, 1984, 2011 by Biblica, Inc.™ Used by permission of Zondervan. All rights reserved worldwide. www.zondervan.com The "NIV" and "New International Version" are trademarks registered in the United States Patent and Trademark Office by Biblica, Inc.™

Copyright © 2019 by Graeme Schultz.

All rights reserved. No part of this publication may be reproduced, distributed or transmitted in any form or by any means, including photocopying, recording, or other electronic or mechanical methods, without the prior written permission of the publisher, except in the case of brief quotations embodied in critical reviews and certain other non-commercial uses permitted by copyright law. For permission requests, write to the publisher, addressed "Permissions Coordinator", at the address below.

Graeme Schultz/Gobsmacked Publishing

19 Trotters Lane
Cudgee, Victoria, Australia, 3265

Email: graeme@design2build.net.au

www.gobsmackedpublishing.com.au

Cataloguing-in-Publication Data:

Author: Schultz, Graeme

Email: graeme@design2build.net.au

Title: As if

Subjects: Devotional

AS IF

Graeme Schultz

ISBN 978-0-6484690-2-5 (paperback)

ISBN 978-0-6484690-3-2 (ebook)

Typeset by bookbound.com.au

Contents

Introduction		vii
Chapter 1	What the Kingdom of God isn't	1
Chapter 2	The better way	4
Chapter 3	My true home	7
Chapter 4	Who gains?	10
Chapter 5	The end of life as we know it	13
Chapter 6	The higher way	16
Chapter 7	Great expectations	19
Chapter 8	The chasm	22
Chapter 9	Life source	26
Chapter 10	Belief	30
Chapter 11	Assurance	33
Chapter 12	The view from the other side	37
Chapter 13	Two truths	40
Chapter 14	The truth about the kingdoms	45
Chapter 15	The veil of this world	49
Chapter 16	Beyond the veil	53
Chapter 17	The cross of Christ	58
Chapter 18	The doing dilemma	62
Chapter 19	The offence of the gospel	65
Chapter 20	Life in the Spirit	68

Chapter 21	God wants me	72
Chapter 22	But do I want God	76
Chapter 23	The true God	79
Chapter 24	The true me	83
Chapter 25	As if	88
Conclusion		93

Introduction

Have you ever wondered why Jesus talked about the Kingdom of God so much?

Sure, it was His home base, and the place where His Father lived, so it held a special place in His heart; but apart from that, it seems like an unusual subject with which to be preoccupied. And He was preoccupied with it. By my count, Jesus referred to the Kingdom of God more than fifty times in the gospels, and the apostles that number again.

If it had been up to me, I would have spent more time talking about the big-ticket items like sin, holy living, worship and prayer. But while Jesus may have touched on these subjects, He always seemed to be distracted by the one subject that really filled His screen, the Kingdom of God. It was like an obsession, an addiction of the best kind—Jesus seemed to be totally distracted by the Kingdom of God.

For most of my life, I wrote it off as simply an unusual turn of phrase that was used in a generic way to encompass all things spiritual—but now, I'm not so sure. Lately I've been wondering if the thing that consumed Jesus is supposed to consume us all, and we can't get a handle on this whole "Christianity thing" unless we get the Kingdom of God resolved for what it truly is.

I'm not suggesting that we can't be saved—that is a gift—but I am suggesting that we can't walk profoundly and deeply in our salvation without grasping what made Jesus tick.

I probably wouldn't even be writing about it now if I hadn't been stopped in my tracks by a time of hardship about a decade ago. That time in my life made me rethink everything. I found myself asking God some questions—questions about how to fix troubling circumstances, and about whether some circumstances were beyond fixing because of the wrong decisions I had made which created them.

There is a lot of ground still to cover in this book, but let me say from the outset that I know now that most of these questions were asked from the perspective of the kingdom of this world. I didn't know how to relate to God as a resident of His kingdom, so my dialogue was an attempt to leap across the great chasm that existed between my world and His.

To be honest, I didn't know that residency in the Kingdom of God was an option for me; nobody told me that I could approach God as a beloved son. I thought the best I could hope for was to serve God to the best of my ability and hope it would be enough to attract His attention.

> *Nobody told me how to live as a son of God.*
> *Maybe nobody knew.*

Maybe we Christians have become so accustomed to yelling out to God across the great chasm that we think it is normal to approach God with uncertainty, normal to invite God into our earthly issues instead of relocating ourselves into the safety of His love.

If these words sound like the ramblings of a religious crank, be patient with me please. I have much to explain, and my words are simple words strung together like a necklace of seashells—I will need all of your tenacity and concentration to make a thing of beauty out of a collection of such ordinary words.

My fear is that I will have written too poorly to convey to you a treasure that is beyond imagination, and that we will arrive at the end of this book without you having crossed over the chasm. I know that in the end it's not up to me; it is only the Holy Spirit who draws us towards the splendour of God's love expressed so completely at the cross of Christ. But I want to do honour to that great love by conveying in simple language a love that is far beyond man-made superlatives.

No easy task.

Paul crafted new words to help him as he attempted to convey that which is beyond human expression: *immeasurable, surpassing, unthinkable*. That is the point for us, too; we must have the courage to push off from the safe harbour of our familiar thinking if we are to discover the lost treasure of God's Kingdom. We know deep down that it is out there; something resonates within us and draws us onward—a memory perhaps, or an ancient longing we can't deny that we were made for the Kingdom of God's love, and we can never be truly satisfied until we are at rest in it.

The chasm that separates the Kingdom of God from the kingdom of this world is impossible to cross by human effort, yet we can be carried over it in an instant if we will change our thinking.

If this book is about anything, it is about crossing that chasm.

Thanks for your patience so far … *stay with me now; the road ahead might get a bit bumpy.*

CHAPTER 1

What the Kingdom of God isn't

I remember hearing a story about two little orphaned girls who were adopted by a Christian couple and lifted out of the hardship of a third world country. They left behind a life of squalor, fear, and hunger, living on the streets, and began a new life in the relative ease and safety of rural Australia.

Their new parents loved and nurtured them as their own. They were embraced into the family household as equal members, with all of the rights and privileges of natural born children. Every day they were treated with love and respect. Meal times, daily activities, and bedtime were all lavish expressions of their new parents' love.

The two environments could not have been more different: now food was plentiful, their home was safe and warm, and the stress of living on the streets was replaced by the kindness and gentleness of two truly good parents.

Yet something wasn't right.

Every day the children would secretly stockpile food under their beds. They took fruit, biscuits, and anything else they could get their hands on, and squirreled them away in preparation for the time when life would revert to the old days.

And perhaps even worse than their compulsion to shore up for their physical needs, they also continued to live in fear. Even though they were treated well by all at home, school and church, they remained emotionally insecure and clung to each other in private, wondering when this temporary nirvana would all come to an end and they would find themselves impoverished and alone all over again.

Their entire environment was bathed in love and security, yet they continued to live as children of another land. But it was all in their heads—they couldn't bring their thinking into agreement with their new environment.

> *A great chasm separated these two environments—*
> *a chasm that was constructed and maintained by their thinking.*

They thought their new home was makeshift, and that their comfort and security could not be counted upon; so they lived in their new home with the mindset of temporary visitors, even though the assurance of permanence was all around them.

Unbeknownst to their new parents, the girls doubted the reality of their new life, and in spite of the promise of a wonderful future, they continued to live by the ways of the past.

They didn't know how to live as children of the promise…just like I didn't know how to live as a son of God. There was no problem with the girls' new home, just as there is no problem with the Kingdom of God. The problem for me, as it was for the two girls, was changing my thinking and learning how to live there.

We cannot bring our old paradigms and habits with us into the Kingdom of God, else we find ourselves behaving like beggars rather than the sons and daughters we really are.

So the problem for us is not that our citizenship in the Kingdom of God is in any way tenuous or conditional, rather it is that we attempt to live in the promises and abundance of God's heart by the means of our old pre-salvation mindset.

We will see God as He really is when we pass through the veil of death, and then the great chasm created by our earthbound thinking will fall away. But for now we must learn to live by faith—not faith generated by self-effort, but a restful faith that God is as good and loving as He claims to be.

> *It is in our hands (and our heads).*

God has transferred us to the Kingdom of His Beloved Son, just as He promised in Colossians 1:3. All that remains is for us to boldly walk in it. Our relocation is complete; we are home where we belong, yet our natural instincts stand in opposition to our new citizenship.

So we circle around and around God's love attempting to bridge the divide by the means we have always employed, yet knowing in our hearts that there is a better way…*if we could only figure it out.*

If only we could learn how to live in this new truth.

CHAPTER 2
The better way

The two little girls brought their old way of thinking to their new home with the result that they enjoyed only a fraction of the potential of their new lives. But they couldn't help it; they had no way of knowing how to think differently. They had been pre-wired by their past to think and live as they did; they had no other previous experience to lean on.

The experience they did have suggested that this time of provision and safety would pass, that it was like every other moment of hope they had ever experienced—it was an illusion, just a passing period of comfort before life exerted its inevitable troubles again…*better to be safe than sorry.*

I can relate to them.

It was not that I experienced the same impoverished past as them, but that my past was impoverished in its own way because life had taught me to think wrongly about the most important thing of all—the heart and nature of God.

I was pre-wired to expect God's favour to be in proportion to my good (or bad) way of life.

The lightbulb moment for me came when I was asking God those questions I referred to earlier: questions about how to fix troubling circumstances, and about whether some circumstances were beyond fixing because of the wrong decisions I had made which created them.

God was silent on the matter.

I think it was because He didn't understand the questions, or at least that they didn't make sense in the context of His Kingdom. And had He answered them in the way I had asked them, He would be validating a way of thinking which was very wrong.

In God's heart, I was asking the wrong questions! They may have been valid for someone still living in the kingdom of this world, but not valid for a son of the Kingdom of Light.

What was wrong with my questions?

They denied the most basic tenet of my citizenship in God's Kingdom.

They implied that the kingdom of this world controlled my future and not the Kingdom of God—in much the same way that the little girls were controlled by their past environment instead of their present one.

Ultimately neither God, nor the children's new parents, can overrule the choices made by one living on the basis of a past truth. In both cases, the old truth had been supplanted by a new one; but the only way the new truth could operate was that it be fully embraced as fact, then the old would fall away and have no place.

For this reason my prayers made no sense to God. He had sent His Son to die and returned me to the Kingdom of His love. He knew that I had received this love gift—yet I continued to think and act as if I was still a foreigner.

This may be a new line of thinking for many readers; it's the bumpy part of the journey I referred to earlier.

I am suggesting that God responds to us according to the Kingdom we choose as our true home, and unfortunately we can't have a bit of each. If we choose to approach God as citizens of the kingdom of this world, then we limit ourselves to the way the world meets needs—in this world it is always on the basis of, and in proportion to, our good (or bad) way of life.

The Kingdom of God doesn't operate that way; God's economy is always on the basis of His unconditional love. Romans 5:8 sums it up for us: "But God demonstrates His own love for us in this: While we were still sinners, Christ died for us". This is how the Kingdom of God works; it is always a demonstration of His love independent of our management of good and evil.

If we choose to rest in that love,
then the abundant life that Jesus came to give us will be ours;
if we choose to bring our virtue to God in order to qualify,
then we will be limited by the ways of the world.

So the question remains: how do we make the Kingdom of God our true habitation?

CHAPTER 3

My true home

Jesus purchased my citizenship in the Kingdom of God on the day when He died on the cross, and I received that gift on the day I accepted Him. From that day on, I have been a son of God with equal rights in God's Kingdom as if I were Jesus Himself.

My citizenship has no price tag associated with it; it is a gift. And similarly my choice to live as a citizen of God's Kingdom has no price tag associated with it; it is all a gift from the extravagance of God.

If I come, cap in hand, to God and ask Him to treat me as a citizen of His Kingdom, even though I am choosing to live and think as a citizen of another kingdom, then I diminish the extravagance of His gift.

He paid the highest of prices so that I would come to Him as a son; anything less than sonship belittles His act of love.

This is not about being haughty or vain; it is about living with respectful boldness in the inheritance Christ won for us. There are already too many puffed up Christians who are full of the importance of their service or ministry; we are simply the objects of God's extravagant love and mercy – nothing more, nothing less.

We don't get to elevate ourselves in the presence of Jesus, yet if we boldly assume upon the outcomes of the cross, we are elevated to greatness through His indwelling.

And that is precisely why Jesus spoke of the Kingdom of God so often; He wanted us to fully partake of the accomplishments of the cross. It is why He came. John 10:10 tells us that "Jesus came that we might have life, and have it abundantly," and it is only in the Kingdom of God that this life can be found. He paid the highest price imaginable so that we would *live* as full-fledged citizens of Heaven.

In the past I had always assumed that Jesus wanted me to live as His humble servant. I thought that humility and a self-deprecating lowliness were the hallmarks of true Christian character, and that the best version of me was coated in a shrinking, bashful modesty.

I had taken the message of God's extravagant love and filtered it through the world's expectations of me, with the result that my citizenship in the Kingdom of God was more shrinking violet than confident son.

Not that God wants me to be brash or proud, but He does want me to walk confidently through life as the object of my Father's extravagant love.

You see, the me that God recreated at the cross is a perfect representation of Himself; I was reborn in God's image just like Adam was in the beginning. And in the same way that God exists in a confident self-assurance of His nature, so also should I. It is all part of the new nature I received in my salvation package, and to live with any sense of reluctance or trepidation is out of character for a son of God who is at home in His Father's kingdom.

My new home does not contain fear, doubt or lack.

Impoverished thinking belongs in the kingdom of this world, but it is completely foreign in God's Kingdom. To doubt our right to walk the halls of Heaven, or recline in the presence of our Father, is so out of place in God's heart that He cannot comprehend or respond to it.

Do you understand what I am saying? There is a sense of assurance that fits the environment of God's Kingdom; it is the same assurance that Jesus has in His Father's house, and it is the correct posture for us to adopt too.

We limit the expression of God's extravagance in our lives when we approach Him as anything less than Jesus, because to do so minimises the accomplishments of the cross.

I hope this is not too much of a bumpy ride for you – but there is no other way to put it. We are either fully in Christ or not in Him at all (there is no middle ground), so we must get comfortable with who we are now that Christ's work on the cross has become the new us.

I live in Heaven … right now.

I am not going there. John 5:24 tells me that "I have crossed over from death to life". That means I am a resident of Heaven right now – no more waiting.

The only question that remains is whether I will actually choose to live there.

CHAPTER 4
Who gains?

As important as it is to acknowledge the sacrifice of Christ as the most selfless act to ever take place in human history, there is another even more important reason why we must embrace the accomplishments of the cross. If we do not, then we restrict our lives to the meagre handouts of the kingdom of this world.

*In other words,
I can only be sustained by the economy of one kingdom.*

This is perhaps the most insidious of Satan's lies – that we should even contemplate the notion of cherry picking from the economies of the kingdom of this world and the Kingdom of Light at the same time is utter foolishness. It was never God's intention that we would consider the natural realm as our source of life once we took up residency in His Kingdom. Everything we need is available to us in God's economy. It says in 2 Peter 1:3, "His divine power has given us everything we need for life and godliness through our knowledge of him who called us by his own glory and goodness".

Not that we cease to work with diligence, but that we rest in God's own words that "he will never leave us or forsake us" – the ultimate provision is God's job, not ours.

Let me give you an example. I know a Christian man who prays to God to bless his business, yet he cheats on his taxes and attempts to beat the system at every opportunity. His problem is not that he sins (we all fail to some degree), but that he has a foot in two kingdoms and expects them both to pay dividends, even though the very life source behind them both is diametrically opposed.

God cannot pour out the blessings of Heaven upon someone who chooses the system of this world as their source and security. Let me say again, this is not about 'sin' it is about attempting to live as a citizen of two kingdoms.

When I choose to cherry pick from both kingdoms according to a blending of my religious leanings and my sense of self-interest, then I inadvertently, and inevitably, choose the lower kingdom as my source. God's hands are tied by my lack of faith in His ability to provide, or perhaps my lack of confidence that His provision will do.

Choosing the economy of this world is not simply about choosing the wrong vocation, which might in some way be opposed to Christian values. Rather, it is choosing to retain our identity as people who live by the economy of good and evil, which Adam gave us, when we have been offered a distinctly different and better way to live.

Adam's economy of good and evil is based on human effort and ingenuity. God's economy of life is based on God's freely given and unconditional love, favour and blessing. We cannot present God with the currency of Adam's economy and expect a heavenly dividend in return; and we cannot seesaw between these two economies as the issues of life demand.

We either trust God, or we don't.

And that was the crossroad that I came to all those years ago: can I trust God with everything? If I can't, then I am effectively trusting Him with nothing.

My Christianity hadn't actually processed that information until that point in time, and so my dual citizenship held me in the grip of the lower economy even though a much better way was available to me. My new economy was about so much more than material provision; it was about my internal sense of wellbeing and security.

So I'm the one who gains!

But only if I am willing to believe that God is as good as He claims to be… otherwise I wait until I die to partake in that which I have had all along.

As I mentioned, this is not about sin – that was dealt with at the cross. This is about our decision to live as citizens of the kingdom that was reopened to us at the cross. Jesus took our sin, but He cannot force us to live with Him as citizens of His kingdom – that decision is up to us.

Many accept their status as citizens of the Kingdom of God in principle, but fail to take up their residency there, choosing to live as Adam's offspring rather than God's. You might wonder how this is even possible. It is possible if we remain dependent on the securities offered by this world when a higher form of security awaits.

In other words, we choose to embrace all of the language and culture of Christianity, without actually leaping across the chasm and hiding our existence in the one to whom the language and culture refers. We are more attached to a system than a person.

This is the great paradox of the Christian faith – that we have been elevated to such a high status by virtue of the blood of Christ, yet we fail to comprehend the scale of the gift that is offered to us. So we find ourselves believing in the claims made by the kingdom of this world to be the source of our daily lives – because these claims are more physically tangible – rather than the claims of the Kingdom of God, which is radically greater yet invisible to the natural eye.

The ultimate outcome is that we live as spiritually impoverished people, just as the two little girls lived as physically impoverished people, all because – like the two little girls – we can't comprehend the magnificence of what we are in.

The challenge for us then is to discover the truth about the Kingdom of God and our status within it, and then to step over the line of our doubt and complacency by relocating our identity and security into it.

It's easier to say than to do, because it is not just another church program or devotional exercise that we might try out for a time – this is the end of our life as we know it. If we take this step, then we are abandoning our old ways and long-held securities and casting ourselves entirely into the care of God… *forever*. No more dipping back into the ways of the past, no more grabbing the steering wheel when life seems to be going off track – *you know what I mean* – but staying the course and trusting that God has our lives held firmly in the safety of His love.

CHAPTER 5

The end of life as we know it

The only way the two little girls could ever truly enjoy their new lives was to let go of the old. Just because they had been physically removed from their impoverishment didn't make it vanish from their conscious thoughts. To be free of the past, they had to choose to leave it behind and fully embrace the new.

This wasn't easy because they didn't know if they could trust the new. They didn't know if it would be true to the promises it made. There was no way to be sure, yet there was a deep yearning to let go and fall into the love of their new parents. They could continue to live in the *hope* that they would be safe in their new world, while discretely stockpiling supplies just in case…but that would be a denial of the truth and such an uncertain way to live.

The same is true of us. We don't know if we can trust the promises made by the Kingdom of God. For this reason, many people live in *hope* that it is all it claims to be, while discretely trusting also in the ways of the world…*just in case the kingdom doesn't deliver as promised.* We have a deep yearning to abandon our fears and reservations and cast our lives headlong into the love of our Heavenly Father, but we are unsure if it will work out, especially considering our past experience.

The failings of the past are a stumbling block for many of us. It was the same for me when I wondered whether some circumstances were beyond fixing because of the wrong decisions I had made which created them. We all make mistakes as we stumble along through life. Some are relatively inconsequential, but others are mammoth – *it's the big mistakes that cause us the most trouble.*

A parking fine or loose word might not cause us much concern, but the big issues like theft, infidelity, time in prison, or taking a life through a car accident can be very hard to get past. Whatever it might be, big or small, the doubts associated with these failings will often attempt to disqualify us from God's promises as we connect our past failings to God's future favour.

It's a big leap to have committed a catastrophic wrongdoing, and then expect to stand before God with our hands out. Yet that is exactly the claim that our salvation makes.

Paul refers to himself as the chief of sinners and the dwelling place of the Spirit of God in almost the same breath – and we also must make the same leap. It is not a matter of pretending that our failings and weaknesses are not real, but rather an acknowledgement that the love of God expressed on the cross of Christ is so staggering that it overshadows even the worst of our lives.

This is the gospel.

Not so much that we love God and try to please Him, but that He loves us with such an unthinkably vast love that our human failings are diminished to irrelevance in the extravagance of His glorious presence.

We cannot step into our citizenship in the Kingdom of God while we deny its fundamental tenets. The Kingdom of God has an atmosphere of God's unconditional love; it is the all-pervading truth of Heaven. If we are to live as citizens of Heaven, we need to personally process the heart of God, accepting our place in it without the addition of any human qualification, and boldly take our seat around the great banquet table of God's love.

There is no other way to live in His kingdom.

This is the end of life as we know it. If we remove the human performance factor from the operation of the love of God, then an entirely new way to live opens up to us. It is a way devoid of doubt and fear, knowing that our security in the extravagant love of God has placed us above the devastation of life's dramas.

Jesus said, "in this world you will have trouble, but take heart I have overcome the world". He wasn't suggesting that life would not throw its worst at us, but that if we hide ourselves in His love it will eclipse the troubles of this life. As difficult as life's circumstances can be, they pale into insignificance compared to the wonder of living as a citizen of Heaven.

Paul said, "For I consider that the sufferings of this present time are not worth comparing with the glory that is to be revealed to us". He wasn't diminishing the struggles of life but magnifying the extraordinary reality and scope of the Kingdom of God.

> *It comes down to where we choose to live,
> and which kingdom will hold us.*

Just like the little girls, we can have all that is contained in our new life handed to us for free; but it will have no more than a superficial benefit unless we allow this new life to hold our identity.

That was my problem, too. I had tried to pull God into my earthly identity by presenting Him with my religious service and good lifestyle, expecting that it would be enough to attract His favour, instead of relocating my identity and confidence into Him, His love, and His Kingdom.

In fact, this new life creates a whole new set of problems if we do not embrace it as the overarching truth of our existence. A partial acceptance of the Kingdom of God may leave us worse off than we were without it (in the present tense), because we know in principle that it contains all we need for life and godliness, yet these things rarely, if ever, materialise.

The point of the Kingdom of God is not so much that we would find answers for our physical and material issues, but that we would discover a life so far above these issues that they pale into insignificance by comparison.

By nature we cannot imagine such a possibility – that we could live amid the storms of life without being smashed by them *simply by resting in the love of God.* But that is the leap we must make, that a higher and better way to live awaits us, if we will only abandon ourselves to it.

CHAPTER 6
The higher way

By now the comparisons between the two little girls and us may be wearing a bit thin, so please indulge me as I continue to make use of them to illustrate the realities of our situation.

It is extremely difficult for us to imagine life other than through our past experience, with the outcome that we inadvertently shape the new out of the old. The two little girls were stuck in this cycle. Unable to grasp that the paradigms of the old had passed away, they continued to live within those paradigms as if they were transferable between the old and the new. They thought that whatever worked in their old environment would work equally well (if not better) in the new one. So instead of begging for food as if it were a rare and unobtainable commodity, they simply stockpiled it as if it were a rare and unobtainable commodity.

Peter's radical statement – "all that we need for life and godliness" is freely and limitlessly available to us at the Father's banqueting table – is an elusive idea when we connect it to our past experience. For this reason, we Christians have a tendency to bring our old mode of operation along with us into God's kingdom. We think this way because we find it hard to come to terms with the notion that we can be satisfied and happy when our earthly circumstances are not as we would like them. It is a self-preservation mode of operation based on the system of this world – a system that declares we cannot be truly content amidst the turmoil of life.

When things get difficult, we are most likely to approach God on the basis of the world's system which measures human worth according to human effort, so at times of need we re-double our efforts to do better in our religious and lifestyle activities in an effort to engage God's help.

And the flip side is that we also try to clean up our lives, hoping that God will be more receptive to a better version of us.

How often have I heard the words, "How can God bless you when you live such a life of sin?" – as if we have the capacity to live such a God-pleasing life that He is *obliged* to reward our good behaviour. None of us can please God by what we do, no matter where we are on the scale of good and evil, so we might as well abandon that approach and discover a better way.

Or perhaps this one: "How can God answer your prayers when you still have unconfessed sin in your life?" – as if God is rendered inert until we utter the word 'sorry'. The word 'sorry' doesn't exist in the Kingdom of God because we are hidden in the perfection of Jesus *(stay with me now)*. Jesus has nothing to apologise for, and He is the new me. And if I trip up, by all means I should apologise to any person affected, but not to God, because that would imply that God thinks the work of Christ is not sufficient to resolve my human condition.

> ***The higher way is preoccupied with the magnificence***
> ***of our union with the indwelling of Christ,***
> ***rather than the mediocrity of our earthly performance.***

The higher way does not attempt to gloss over our human failings; they are just as real now that we are saved as they were before. People who declare that they haven't sinned for years need a reality check; there will always be things we could do or say better, and there will always be room for improvement.

And that's just the point; our salvation was never meant to be all about improving our performance in the theatre of this physical world – *that is a side issue*. It has always been about relocating us to another kingdom where our performance, lifestyle and behaviour are not the measure of our worth; the unconditional love of God is. And the follow-on from that is that God is unable to be all that He wants to be for us as long as we insist on presenting our personal best to Him as the means of releasing His unconditional love.

In the case of the two little girls, they not only lived their own lives with an impoverished mindset, but they also restricted their new parents from expressing the extent of their selfless love. The new parents could only provide the supply necessary for the girl's physical needs for that day and to stockpile for the future, but they wanted to give them so much more

– they wanted the girls to abandon themselves into the extravagance of their love.

You know where I am going with this; God cannot be true to His extravagant love for us if we choose to limit it by making it conditional on our performance, no matter how spiritual our performance might be. If we add conditions to an expression of love that is unconditional, then it is no longer the same expression of love, and in the case of God's love – is it the opposite. God cannot reshape His nature to suit our insecurities, even if they are well intentioned.

And the Kingdom of God cannot operate according to our pre-determined ways just because we are too insecure or stubborn to change. God changes not, and His Kingdom changes not – we are the ones who need to get with the program.

CHAPTER 7
Great expectations

Jesus seemed to have an expectation for His disciples, which they continually fell short of. One in particular comes to mind in Mark 4:35-41:

> *That day when evening came, he said to his disciples, 'Let us go over to the other side.' Leaving the crowd behind, they took him along, just as he was, in the boat. There were also other boats with him. A furious squall came up, and the waves broke over the boat, so that it was nearly swamped. Jesus was in the stern, sleeping on a cushion. The disciples woke him and said to him, 'Teacher, don't you care if we drown?' He got up, rebuked the wind and said to the waves, 'Quiet! Be still!' Then the wind died down and it was completely calm. He said to his disciples, 'Why are you so afraid? Do you still have no faith?' They were terrified and asked each other, 'Who is this? Even the wind and the waves obey him!'*

I had always thought Jesus was a bit harsh on this occasion. The disciples were simply responding to the conditions around them; they didn't even know it was possible to command the wind and waves to calm down. Yet Jesus didn't see it that way; in His mind, the security of being in his Father's kingdom was much greater than the impending storm, and He saw no reason why the disciples didn't have the same perspective.

Jesus simply expected the Kingdom of God to operate according to the laws, which controlled it. Not laws like the Ten Commandments or the road laws, but laws more like the law of gravity. It was a principle that was always 'on', no conditions to be met – just use it at will.

And Jesus knew it was always on for us too.

The disciples didn't get it until the Holy Spirit removed the veil from their eyes on the day of Pentecost, then they really discovered what they had gotten into. Peter was so galvanised by this experience that it changed his perspective in one fell swoop – he realised that the flow was always on for him too, and he preached as a transformed man.

Peter became a man whose expectations mirrored the nature of the Kingdom of God – his expectations shifted away from himself and his own abilities, to the Kingdom of God and its abilities. He aligned himself with the higher truth that defined him now that he was a citizen of God's kingdom, and he switched from the impoverishment of self-effort to the extravagance of participating in Spirit-energized kingdom life.

All of this was equally available to Peter back when the storm hit the boat – it's just that his past experience hid it from him. Jesus could see it quite clearly, He could see that Peter had the same ability to calm the storm as He did, and He could see that Peter had the same ability to rest in the security of His Father's love too.

The Holy Spirit displays to us the real truth of our existence in Christ. John 15:26 tells us "the Spirit testifies about Jesus" and that was what Peter experienced, the Holy Spirit revealed to him a reality so superior to his previous understanding that it transformed him from the inside out.

The same is true of us.

When we see the spectacular reality of our new home in the Kingdom of God, we can choose to make this reality our day-to-day truth. The choice is ours, not God's. God can't force us to live as citizens of His kingdom in the present tense. If we choose to delay until we pass over at death, then that is up to us – all He can do is reveal the stunning accomplishments of the blood of Christ and invite us to participate.

You might remember earlier in this book where I referred to God's silence with respect to my prayers that didn't reflect my true (kingdom) status. All God can do is reveal to us the truth of who and what we are as a result of the cross of Christ – and He can only respond to us according to the faith in Christ that we bring to Him.

The faith of a beggar is a far cry from the faith of a son.

The little girls approached their new home as beggars with the result that they could only receive material supply – when in reality, their real and most profound need was that they discover the security that can be fulfilled only by love. Their impoverished mindset kept out the thing they needed most, because their past experience convinced them that it was better to have physical nourishment, even if it meant doing without the nurture of love.

Their need for survival was so great that it eclipsed everything else – even love.

We tend to approach God in the same way; we elevate the needs of this earthly life above our need to hide ourselves in His unconditional love. In fact, hiding ourselves in God's love is such an unfamiliar concept that we pay it no more than lip service and turn our attention to the seemingly more pressing issues of shoring up our physical lives.

In Luke 10:20, on the occasion when the disciples were amazed that even the demons were subject to them, Jesus said, "Nevertheless, don't rejoice in this, that the spirits are subject to you, but rejoice that your names are written in heaven". He was pointing out to the disciples the correct order of things – our citizenship in Heaven is greater than the happenings of our earthly lives (no matter how spiritual they might seem).

Our citizenship in God's Kingdom is an end unto itself, not merely a means of fixing the issues we confront on a daily basis. This is the chasm we must cross over – that God Himself is the prize, not the things we need Him to provide so that we can get through life.

It is a shift in expectations. From the meagre expectations of the provision of our earthly needs, to the great expectation of knowing God and His vast heart of love – that discovery is the essence of life in the Kingdom of God.

CHAPTER 8
The chasm

Many Christians will agree in principle with the sentiments expressed in the previous chapter. We give our approval to the notion that the cross of Christ is the object and focus of our faith, yet we actually live our lives in conflict with that fact. We find it difficult to escape the pull of our doubts that life will be okay, and that God has 'got us', and so we dip our toes in the Kingdom of God (as the need arises), instead of firmly planting both feet there.

In that regard, we have retained Adam's definition of God, a definition which reflects Adam's independent old nature. This Old Nature assumes the need to present God with our personal best to somehow attract His favour. Instead we must redefine God to align with the truth that recognises our reunion with Him, a union that is not based on our best efforts – but God's love.

> *Our only way of escape is to take the big leap –*
> *the leap into the fact that 'God has got us'.*

As I said, many agree in principle, and as a result they assume that the leap is already behind them. However they may have simply resolved their eternal destiny rather than their present tense citizenship. John 1:12 sums it up for us: "Yet to all who received Him, to those who believed in His name, He gave the right to become children of God". When we receive Jesus we are presented with the right to be God's children. Many resolve their eternal destiny by believing in Jesus, but don't realize that they can also exercise the right to actually live in the 'here and now' as God's sons and daughters.

Living as God's children is so much more than adopting the well-used language of Christianity.

I mentioned earlier that it is the end of life as we know it – and it is!

Imagine the moment in time when you first received Jesus into your life. There were some very personal and perhaps emotional things happening which registered in your conscious mind.

Going deeper into the realm of the Spirit a dramatic scene was also taking place, and I will use some theatrical licence to describe it.

As your spirit becomes aware of the presence of the Holy Spirit, a spontaneous dialogue begins to unfold regarding any questions or comments you may have. You start by outlining your intention to get the repentance process underway as soon as possible as there is quite a bit to cover. Early memories going all the way back to childhood failures crowd your thoughts and tumble out in a tangle of regrets.

The Holy Spirit gives you a few minutes to run out of steam and then clarifies something you had never really understood. Repentance is not about a list, it is about a life – it is not a record of mistakes made, but the life source behind those mistakes. If it were simply a matter of reciting a record of wrong doings, and then saying sorry, it would never end; there would always be more to add to the end of the list. Making mistakes is the normal expression of the fallen human condition; and we, as a race, are therefore defined by failure.

Repentance is turning away from one life source and toward a new one, it is letting go of the life source that Adam handed to us, and embracing the life source that Jesus gives. The problem then, is the life source, not the list of wrongdoing produced by that life source. There is actually only one item on the list – will I choose Christ and His work on the cross as the source of my being and abandon my old self-made existence?

Separately repenting of individual sins is like hopping on one foot – it keeps us busy, but gets us nowhere. There is always more hopping to do, more sins to regret, more memories of failures to resolve.

Wouldn't it be better to cut off the life source that continues to build up the list?

The Holy Spirit has a good imagination; think of it this way, He says:

You have an earring clipped to each ear. These earrings are like alligator clips, the kind that you attach to a car battery. One side is positive and the other negative. These alligator clips have leads that go all the way back to the Tree of the Knowledge of Good and Evil. They are your life source in so far as they deliver to you a constant evaluation of how you are doing based on your management of good and evil (positive and negative). Satan doesn't care if you do good or evil; he just wants you to gain your identity and confidence from what you do. He wants you striving to build up the good side of the ledger and avoiding bad deeds, so that your eyes will always be fixed on your own performance.

Even though you are a Christian and have been saved by the blood of Jesus, you continue to look to the wrong tree as your source of life. You determine your worth according to your personal performance, rather than the gift of life Jesus gave to you.

It's like hopping in one spot; you never actually get to the point where anything changes.

Next the Holy Spirit asks you if you would like to try a new life source – the unconditional love of God expressed so completely on the cross.

You say 'Yes, of course'; and the Holy Spirit removes the alligator clips from your ears and tells you to stand back. He brings the positive and negative terminals together and causes a massive short circuit down along the leads and through the whole system. The positive and negative deeds generated over your whole life converge on the Tree of the Knowledge of Good and Evil; and, in one mighty explosion, the tree is blown to a million pieces. As far as you are concerned, the tree no longer exists; it can no longer contribute to your sense of worth.

The Tree of the Knowledge of Good and Evil is dead to you.

Then the Holy Spirit asks if you are ready for the really good part. He tells you to close your eyes and hold out your hands – into each hand he places a huge insulated cable, like the kind you see in a power station. The cables are connected to a very big switch, which is the cross of Christ, and beyond that switch the cables go all the way to the throne of God. The Holy Spirit asks one more time if you are ready, and when you nod your head, He winks at Jesus who then closes the switch.

You are immediately flooded with all of the righteousness of God, your spirit is so perfected by this that you become welded – spirit to Spirit – with the very heart of the Father. The Holy Spirit wants to be sure you understand the scale of the thing that has just happened, so he asks you to look at your hands. As you look down, you see nail holes in your hands and realise you have been crucified with Christ. You have been reconnected to the Heavenly Father through the cross of Christ; all of the love and life in the Kingdom of God are now yours. You are the same as Adam was, at the very beginning before sin.

The Holy Spirit looks you in the eye and asks, "Do you want to be in this perfect union with your Father for all eternity?" As you say yes, he slips a bolt through the cables and into the nail holes in your hands, then tightens the nut and smiles – now you know that He will never leave you nor forsake you. Your eternal union is held in place by the continuously flowing righteousness of Jesus.

His love is yours forever, His life is yours for all eternity, and He has bound Himself to you.

> **You have been connected to a new life source;
> the old is gone forever.**

This bond cannot be broken by good and evil, as it is not related to your performance. The bond is held in place by God's love, not our management of the issues of life. The chasm is crossed by God's initiative; all we do is give Him permission to take our old life source away, and replace it with His freely given divine nature.

As I said, a bit of poetic licence, but you get the idea.

CHAPTER 9
Life source

From the perspective of the physical realm, the dramatic change within us barely causes a ripple in our consciousness. That is because it is primarily not about the physical realm; it is an event that occurred in the spiritual realm. It has roll-on effects in our physical lives on planet earth, but it is primarily about something far more important than the circumstances and issues we face here.

That's not to say that it has no relevance until we die. In fact, quite the contrary is true – it impacts our daily lives in the most profound and tangible ways imaginable. But rather, those tangible impacts are the result or *overflow* of this momentous spiritual event, and so it is important that we understand what that event looks like so we can bring our physical lives into alignment with it.

Harking back to the two little girls, they didn't bring their lives into alignment with the dramatic event that had taken place. Instead, they continued to live in alignment with their previous condition, with the result that their physical impoverishment continued to rule over them and their circumstances.

The scale of the change that has occurred to us is beyond description – yet for most of my life I lived as if it was more theoretical that real.

In Ephesians 1:18 Paul prays that the eyes of our hearts would be enlightened in order that we might see the stunning accomplishments of the cross of Christ, in and for us. He didn't pray that God would complete a dramatic change in our lives, but rather that we would simply see the change that has already been completed. He didn't ask God to do anything except let the light in, and once the light of God's love and power (in us) registers in all its glory, we can finally choose to leave behind our old source of life.

What does this realignment to a new life source actually look like?

Good question!

Our new life source is already fully engaged into us as declared in 2 Peter 1:4, which says, "Through these He has given us His great and precious promises, so that through them you may participate in the divine nature". Our part is to align our thinking with this new reality *(we are now able to participate in the divine nature).* If we fail to do that, we will continue to think as if we were still in our old condition.

So the realignment is all about choosing to believe.

John puts it so beautifully in John 20:31 where he expresses the reason why he wrote his gospel. "But these things are written that you may *believe* that Jesus is the Christ, the Son of God, and that by believing you may *have life* in His name".

> ***In other words, you get "life"***
> ***by believing that Jesus gave you life.***

Sometimes we attempt to get God to give us what we want by presenting Him with something other than belief – perhaps hope, or persistence, or assertive or spiritual behaviour; but God has made it quite clear that we participate in God's divine life by believing – not in God (that is a given), but believing that the blood of Christ qualifies us to participate in everything that was accomplished for us at the cross.

If we don't believe that the blood of Christ has qualified us to participate in the divine nature, then we will continue to live and think as Adam did, *hoping* that God will be pleased with us because of what we are doing.

I often hear Christians speaking of their disdain for religion, yet subtly, by expecting God to respond to our personal best, we epitomise religion – because that is what religion is, performing a manmade activity to get a divine response.

The belief that God actually requires is devoid of human virtue; it clings to the grace of God without the addition of human effort of any kind, it trusts that God wants me, and that He has got me – and it rests there.

This resting in the character of God is the great chasm that stretches before the believer like the Grand Canyon. We cannot cross it by human effort; it can be traversed only by leaning into the grace of God.

Would any sane person lean over the Grand Canyon? Certainly not! It would be the most reckless of acts – yet, that is belief. That belief is so convinced that God has got us that it leans into Him in spite of all of the contrary natural evidence.

Peter did it when Jesus came walking on the water. He stepped out into the impossible, and then began to sink when the natural evidence imposed itself upon his mind. The natural evidence will always attempt to discredit our confidence in God, so that in the end we are left with neither belief nor unbelief, and just find ourselves wallowing in the shallows of well-intentioned hope.

To realign ourselves to a new life source, we must believe unequivocally that it is a fact. Not merely a theological truth that we accept intellectually or as a broad ideal, but a personal truth in which we have such certainty that we cast ourselves unreservedly into its fidelity.

I have a Christian friend who asked me recently, "What if it's not all true?" He was attempting to believe on the basis of intellectually defensible evidence. But intellectual belief is not belief at all; it is simply a fact that is accepted on account of the physical proof.

True belief is anchored in the Word of God as expressed in the Bible and by the Holy Spirit. Physical evidence is unnecessary. We believe simply because God said so.

Yet this belief is not reckless; it is not the stuff of ever-zealous ambition or self-generated guts and determination. True belief examines the cross of Christ from every angle. It looks at the claims it makes about its accomplishment in restoring our union to Father God, and it casts off all reservation to wholly embrace that truth.

Do not attempt to leap across that chasm without a thorough examination of the cross of Christ. It is a personal thing; we must grasp the scale of its transformation in us and embrace its claims because we are so convinced of it *that we would be foolish to do anything less.*

This conviction is not found in our engagement in the culture and community of Christianity. That follows later. First we must stand alone at the cross and determine if we are personally ready to believe as an individual.

That is the kind of believing John was talking about. That is the kind of believing that receives the life of Jesus.

Don't leave home without it.

CHAPTER 10

Belief

Belief is perhaps the most talked about subject in all Christendom.

Yet it seems to have been presented as something we generate from within ourselves, and if that is the case, then it is no different to any other self-generated activity we perform in Adam's footsteps.

Belief is not primarily something we self-generate that produces an action; it is a conviction that arises from seeing a new truth.

We come to that conviction because the Holy Spirit has done in us what He said He would do, which is reveal the testimony of Jesus (John 15:26). And repentance is turning our lives over to that conviction.

Imagine yourself as a glass of water; you contain the all good and evil of your life. The water you contain is a murky mixture of everything you have ever done. You want to present your best to God to receive His favourable response so you repent of all the evil, even attempting to cover those things you have missed or been unaware of by confessing unknown sins.

The water quality seems to improve a bit, but it is still a long way off the clear, pure water you know God requires. So you add various water purifying processes in addition to repentance like prayer, Bible study, service, worship, etc. only to find that they don't actually improve your water quality.

You look around and see many very murky glasses of water and conclude that you are not so bad after all, so you approach God in the hope that He will recognise your good intentions and respond accordingly.

That is not belief.

At best, that is self-belief, mixed with hope.

Our only option is to empty the container completely and start afresh.

The Holy Spirit did this for us when He disconnected us from the Tree of the Knowledge of Good and Evil. He removed the alligator clips, which had filled us with lies, a murky mix of good and evil thoughts and deeds. He cut off this flow, which was contaminated by human imperfections, and poured the contents down the drain.

And we found ourselves standing before God empty.

There was nothing at all left to present to God – not one good thing to offer Him.

God smiled and said, "At last! I can finally fill you up with My divine nature. Now there is room for Me in you. My desire is that I would fill you with water that is cleaner and purer than you have ever known. It is the life that flows from the very throne of Heaven".

Would you like to be filled with that life now?

This was a crossroad for me because I was not sure how to live without my personal best giving me confidence and security. I was not sure if being empty of self would work for me. But I had to admit to myself that it wasn't actually working very well so far. My confidence in myself had been shaky and my self-security hadn't really felt very secure at all.

So I finally decided, "Yes, I want to be filled with Your life.

That's when the Holy Spirit attached those big cables to my hands through the holes that appeared when I was co-crucified with Christ, and all of the pure, clean life of Heaven surged through my spirit, making me whole.

That is true belief –
it is simply accepting God's life.

All of Him, none of me.

It is not a cocktail of my personal best and God's divine nature. Rather, it is the pure, unadulterated perfection of God, His nature poured into me and filling me to overflowing. I don't want to dilute this purity by mixing in my own attempts at righteous living. I want to live from the purest life source possible – the very heartbeat of God.

This is belief; it is trusting that the life of God in me is enough. To quote Peter, "that it is enough to provide me with all I need for life and godliness".

I continue to be me, and I continue to live responsibly and well, but my lifestyle no longer contributes to my security or identity. Now I am as humanity was first designed to be – *the nature of God living in the form of man.*

This is believing as God first intended it be. It is a restful assurance that God can be trusted with everything…*everything.*

In the same way that nobody taught me how to be a son of God, nobody taught me how to believe either – at least not in the way I have just described. There was plenty of pious talk and lots of enthusiasm for meetings and programs, but when you came right down to it, the believing part was mostly speculation based on the language of the Christian culture in that time and place.

This is not a criticism of any person or group in particular. None of us knew any better. We were all doing our best and hoping that God was happy with it.

I had to learn to believe all by myself.

To some extent we all do.

If we find ourselves in a Christian environment where this kind of believing is the norm, then we may make the leap a little more easily. But in the end there are no shortcuts; we must each look Jesus in the eye and declare, "I am putting my entire existence into Your care".

To do less means that we don't really believe He is all He claims to be.

CHAPTER 11

Assurance

In the past I had looked for my assurance of salvation in the same place where I looked for my other assurances – in the realm of physical evidence.

I looked to my emotional stability and my personal circumstances to determine if God was there, and if my connection to Him was strong.

More often than not, these provided me with a mixed bag. Some things were in order and some weren't, so my assurance was limited. I had inadvertently been using the system handed to me by Adam to validate the new life I had received through Christ.

Let me explain.

My circumstances are the earth-based environment that has been constructed out of the outcomes of humanity's connection to the Tree of the Knowledge of Good and Evil, and my emotional stability is my response to those circumstances. These circumstances ebb and flow. That is the nature of life on earth – even Jesus said, "In this world you will have trouble".

I had assumed that the sense of well-being I experienced when my circumstances were in order was the measure of whether God was pleased with me. In other words, if I felt good, then I was in a good place with God. And if my circumstances were not so good, then I needed to quickly check my connection to God.

Unfortunately my circumstances were not always good (in the world I did have trouble), yet His Word declared loud and clear that He would never leave me nor forsake me. So I found that my circumstances were an unreliable measure of the presence of God in my life, and it also followed that the emotions that resulted from my circumstances were also an unreliable measure of the presence of God in my life.

Jesus went on to say "…but take heart, I have overcome the world".

Did He mean that He had overcome my circumstances?

Not at all. He meant that He had overcome the world order that produced them, He had disconnected me from the Tree of the Knowledge of Good and Evil. He meant that He had opened up to me a new way to live that was radically superior to the hold that the circumstances of this world had over me.

Take a moment to consider that!

This radically superior way to live did not look for its assurance in my physical environment. Instead, it fixed its gaze on one thing only – the cross of Christ – and rested secure in it.

This new way to live contained a new form of evidence to measure its confidence, no longer looking to the random issues of life on earth to validate it – but now looking to our residency within the Kingdom of God as the measure of our well-being.

My earthly circumstances were brought into subjection to the much higher truth of my eternal condition. This placed things into order; my eternal position was made superior to my mortal position – so that now faith overcomes fear, and confidence overcomes doubt.

Jesus also said, "You are not of the world any more than I am of this world" – He was declaring an eternal truth over the disciples which they would realise after He had gone back to His Father. We don't generally perceive ourselves from this perspective; we are more likely to consider the physical truth of our earthly circumstances to be more real and relevant than our new eternal home.

Like the two little girls, we are more easily defined by our past than our present. And we are also more easily defined by our physical circumstances than our Father's love for us. So the Scripture in Hebrews 11:1 must come into play, "Now faith is the assurance of things hoped for" – faith takes hope, and turns it into certainty.

It is not enough to hope that we are saved, nor is it enough to hope that God is with us and will be there in our time of need. Hope leaves us unsatisfied; it is always future-focused and uncertain.

Faith on the other hand is always present tense; it transfers the thing that we hope for out of the future and into the present – because faith rests in the accomplishments of Christ and not the frailty of our earthly performance or circumstances.

We must leave behind the mindset of Adam if we are to have assurance.

Adam connected his spiritual well-being to his earthly performance. We must abandon his thinking and embrace the radical notion that our spiritual well-being is found only in God's unconditional gift of love.

Until we make our earthly performance the *overflow* of the security we have found in God's unconditional love rather than the basis for it, we will continue to swing our gaze back onto our circumstances and ourselves to determine our assurance of salvation. So we must retrain ourselves to think in a way that is contrary to our past thinking and opposed to the thinking of the vast majority of humanity.

> *We must consider ourselves*
> *to be more the product of Christ's sacrifice*
> *than our activities,*
> *which made it necessary in the first place.*

Do you feel a resistance rising up within you to this way of thinking? If so, be assured that this is the normal human condition. In my case, I found my old thinking asserting itself against the work of Christ initially too. It just seemed like too big a stretch to minimize my behaviour and lifestyle to that extent, as if by doing so I would devalue common decency and goodness as fundamentals of the Christian walk.

Yet it is necessary for us to resolve with absolute clarity that the source of our identity and security is independent from our earthly performance if we are to arrive at the full assurance we desire. Our identity and security has been so completely founded in our earthly performance ever since Adam took leave of the presence of God that we can no longer imagine any alternative way to live. Yet that alternative way is the life for which we were made, and re-made again by the blood of Christ.

This is not about abandoning a life founded on good principles and right living, but rather acknowledging that these are meant to be the overflow of Christ within us, rather than the outcome of our independent best efforts.

So the point is that we must learn to rest in Christ. And when we rest in Christ, assurance overflows us like a flood, instead of the trickle from the rusty old garden tap of our good works.

We were designed for assurance; it is the spiritual instinct re-birthed into us by Jesus.

The hosts of Heaven are assured of our salvation as they behold the stunning work completed in us by the cross of Christ, and now we too can change our minds and agree with all that is so obvious in the spiritual realm, instead of the inferior evidence of our daily lives here in the natural realm.

CHAPTER 12

The view from the other side

If we could perceive the same reality that the angels in Heaven do, then we would abandon all our reservations in a heartbeat. Our problem is not the reality itself, but our ability to see it.

The angels in Heaven are so completely informed about the transformation that has been wrought in us by the blood of Jesus, that they are stunned by the meagre response it generates. They watched as the deception of Adam by Satan brought humanity into impoverishment, and they also observed our total release from that impoverished state by the sacrifice of Jesus. They can see a reality which is astonishing in its scope and potential, a reality which has made its home in us, and they long for the day when we will see it to.

The Scriptures speak of the anticipation that is built into creation as it awaits the revealing of the sons of God. This built-in anticipation was activated when Jesus released us from the impoverishment of living under the rule of Satan. The whole of creation can see this and awaits the moment when we also will see it as it really is and abandon our lives to it.

We human beings are without doubt the most extravagant expression of the creative heart of God because we are designed to be perfectly joined and inhabited by His holy nature. The angelic hosts are servants created to do God's bidding, but we are sons and daughters of the Living God, created to freely express the heart of God as the spontaneous overflow of His presence in us.

All of creation can see this – when will we?

Yet we live out our days on earth as if we are still trapped within the limitations of Adam's legacy.

Reality is like that; it is fabricated out of the beliefs we hold to be true.

If the veil of this natural world were drawn away, we would see an entirely different view. We would see the perfect condition we received from Jesus that enables us to walk boldly up to the throne of God, we would see the glory and love that streams constantly from the heart of God into our innermost being, and we would see the flow of divine life that now floods our entire existence – all of this we will see when the veil is drawn up.

And we will also see that this is as real for us now as it will be when we close our eyes for the last time and pass out of this life, the only thing that will change in that moment in time is our sight.

At the present time we may not be able to see God or the angels (or even the demons for that matter). The veil of the natural realm hides them from view (but for the rare exception). We can, however, see all that we need to see with the eyes of our hearts.

In Ephesian 1:18 Paul prays that the eyes of our hearts would be enlightened… so it must be possible to have such sight or else he wouldn't have prayed for it. But what exactly is that sight and how do we activate it?

The heart referred to is our inner man or spirit. It is the real me. My spirit has eyes to see spiritual things (not with physical eyes, but a spiritual vision); it perceives the same truth as the hosts of Heaven. That's why Paul prays that the eyes of our hearts would be enlightened; he wants us to perceive a reality outside of the one perceived by our five senses...he wants us to see the truth as God sees it.

> ***Without that truth,***
> ***we remain bound by the inferior truth of Adam's world.***

Yes, they are both truths – yet only one transcends the natural realm and opens up to us the life of God. Only one of these truths has trading power in the Kingdom of God. We cannot operate as citizens of the Kingdom of God using the principles of the lesser kingdom of this world.

The little girls had two truths to choose between too. One related to life lived according to the principles of this world; it was a life of self-preservation. The other related to life lived in the assurance of their parents' love; it was a life sustained by a great love provided by generous parents.

The two little girls were blinded to this love by their past experiences, and we too are blinded to the sustaining power of the love of God by our past reliance on the Tree of the Knowledge of Good and Evil.

All of Heaven can see this as plain as day.

And we can too – by faith.

We can see the same reality as the angels do – with the eyes of our hearts. The angels could see that the disciples had the ability to calm the storm, they understood Jesus' rebuke completely – it was so obvious to them. They could see that Peter was able to walk on water long before he stepped out of the boat, and they could see that handkerchiefs and aprons that Paul touched could bring healing to the sick.

And they can see that we also are filled with such a remarkable presence of God that all things are possible for us – but only if we will change our view of reality and agree with God.

I have mentioned miraculous events to illustrate this point, events which defied the laws of nature. It is equally nature defying to entrust our entire existence into the care of God. It is exactly the same life source that Jesus used to calm the storm that will also carry us through the storms of life. It is the same life source that raised Jesus from the dead that will sustain us through all that life throws at us.

But only if we will agree with God's view of things.

We cannot have it both ways. We either trust in God or in ourselves and the world in which we live.

God does not respond to hope, desperation or religion. He responds to the perfect sacrifice of Christ, and us too when we put our faith in it.

That's the way He planned things in the beginning, He intended that we would hide ourselves in His great love for us – that we would live by faith in the fact that He will never leave us nor forsake us.

God cannot force us to have faith; it is ours to choose.

CHAPTER 13
Two truths

Is truth absolute?

For instance: It is true that water boils at 100 degrees Celsius – but is it always true?

The answer is that it's true on planet earth, but not on Venus where the atmospheric pressure is different. On the surface of Venus, water boils at about 190 degrees Celsius. So truth is absolute within the context that applies to it.

Can a new truth be created, or is truth a forever thing?

On 3 December 1976 a new truth was created; this truth had never existed before that day. On that day I married my wife, and a new truth came into existence. I was now in union with someone who loved me so much that she wanted to be with me for life – a new world order had arrived.

This new truth was absolute (we are still happily married 42 years later), but it did not exist prior to that date. I adjusted my life to that truth; it changed everything – from my daily routines, to meals, furniture, clothing and ultimately children and grandchildren. Had this new truth not appeared, I would be a completely different person today.

Two truths were available to me on 3 December 1976 – I could stay as I was and live as a product of my past truth, or I could align myself with the new truth… *fortunately for me, I did the latter.*

When Adam and Eve ate from the Tree of the Knowledge of Good and Evil, they created a new truth. This new truth was that their worth would now be determined according to their management of good and evil. This truth was actually true. It wasn't a figment of their imagination; it was a fact – albeit a lesser fact than their previous source of worth. Adam and Eve were now stuck for life in a system that responded to them according to how well they balanced good and evil; it was all about self-generated righteousness.

This system then went on to generate another new truth – religion.

The new truth called religion was also true; it did not exist before it was generated by the Tree of the Knowledge of Good and Evil, but since then it has been an undisputable fact. This new truth provided a means of measuring humanity's management of good and evil. It too was not a figment of their imagination; it was simply a daily reality of life – a new world order had arrived.

Sometimes a truth exists side-by-side with another higher truth and is subject to the higher truth. Birds can fly, but eventually the law of gravity will pull them back to earth. Both are true, but the higher truth (or law) is the prevailing reality.

In Romans 8:2 Paul says, "For in Christ Jesus the law of the Spirit of life has set you free from the law of sin and death". The law of the Spirit of life and the law of sin and death are both truths, but the law of the Spirit of life is the higher and greater truth.

I say all of this to illustrate the fact that there are different ways to live, and different truths to live under as the prevailing fact of our lives. The law of the Spirit of life has set us free from the law of sin and death, but God can't force us to live free – only we can make that decision.

It's like a line in the sand; on one side is the law of the Spirit of life, and on the other side is the law of sin and death – and God says, "Take your pick". He won't force us to live a certain way, He has created us as people with a free will, and He won't insist on what is best for us if we don't choose it. It is the same scenario as the Garden of Eden. The two trees existed side by side, and God allowed Adam and Eve the right to choose who they would be and which truth would prevail in their lives. They determined to live according to the law of sin and death, instead of the Spirit of life.

God warned them that the Tree of the Knowledge of Good and Evil had a down side (death), and that the Tree of Life would provide them with a continuous season of His life-giving love – but they chose to be their own god and self-manage their righteousness… *and God didn't get in the way.*

> **The problem for many is that they choose to**
> **live according to the law of sin and death,**
> **while expecting the outcomes of the law of the Spirit of life.**

They attempt to stand on the wrong side of the line and pull, beg and cajole God into giving them the fruits of the other side. They attempt to live as citizens of the kingdom of this world and still participate in the bounty that is in the Kingdom of God.

The laws that govern life in the kingdom of this world are different than the laws that govern life in the Kingdom of God (like water boiling at different temperatures). We must realign ourselves to the realities of this new Kingdom if we want the outcomes it offers.

I'm not talking about making behavioural changes, but changes in the way we perceive the unconditional love of God. The unconditional love of God is the very atmosphere of the Kingdom of God, and it is important that we come to terms with it.

God will not remake the nature of His love to suit our desire to have it on our own terms; we are the ones who need to remake our thinking to become partakers of it. We can only be partakers in the love of God according to the law of the Spirit of life.

> ***I have said earlier that this is not about salvation;***
> ***it is about learning to live in that salvation***
> ***according to the heartbeat of God,***
> ***rather than the insecurities of Adam.***

On the day when I received Jesus into my life, a new truth overwhelmed and saturated my existence – the unconditional love of God. It was actually a very old truth, as ancient as God Himself; but it was new for me, as I had never known it before. On that day, God gave Himself into eternal union with me, and He gave me all of the bounty and wonders of His Kingdom too.

There was just one condition, that I embrace it as my sole source of life.

I had to let go of the past to embrace the future; I couldn't have a handhold on each.

I had to decide which truth would be the life-sustaining fact of my existence – God's love or my self-management of life. I had to square up to the claims of the cross and determine once and for all that the love of God was enough to carry me through everything.

You see, the truth that I could be sustained by my personal management of good and evil was a truth which could operate only within the context that applied to it – that context is the earthly realm. If I expected the outcomes of the cross of Christ to apply to my life, then I had to choose to live in the context in which they applied – the Kingdom of God.

The purpose of the sacrifice of Jesus is that I would be rescued from the dominion of darkness and brought into the Kingdom of the beloved Son of God (Colossians 1:13). Within this new context is contained an absolute truth – the truth that I am a joint heir with Christ to all that the Kingdom holds. But I cannot take possession of this inheritance as a citizen of another realm – I must cancel that citizenship and transfer my allegiance and confidence across to the Kingdom of God.

In the same way that we would not lightly cancel our earthly citizenship from the country of our birth to a new and distant country, we cannot lightly transfer our citizenship across to the Kingdom of God. Some people lack sufficient confidence in the potential of their new country to provide for them that they maintain dual citizenship – they remain citizens of both the old and the new.

Recently in Australia a number of politicians had to revoke the citizenship of their birth and retain their Australian citizenship only in order to be permitted to function in their public role. Similarly, dual citizenship does not work in the context of the Kingdom of God either. We are either all in or all out. When we die, our citizenship in the kingdom of this world will automatically fall away, and we will find ourselves to be citizens of one realm only; but until that day, we must choose where we will live.

It is a faith choice.

This faith choice is not lightly made. It is not a matter of jumping on board with the latest program or getting pumped up by the newest worship video. In fact, this faith choice is unlike all of my previous attempts to engage the presence of God into my life, because it is the end of my life as I have known it.

One does not lightly put an end to all we have known;
we are too invested to let go so easily.

The primary difference between Christians who have transferred their entire identity over to the Kingdom of God and those who attempt to hold dual citizenship is related to how we understand the operation of God in our lives. A Christian with dual citizenship has to pull the blessings and favour of God across the chasm between these two kingdoms. It is a case-by-case involvement of God in the issues of their lives that is dependent on prayer and other spiritual activities. A believer who takes this approach attempts to engage God into the issues of their residency in the natural realm, and so blessings are perceived as individual events rather than a continual state of their existence.

A Christian who has transferred their identity to the Kingdom of God does not have to pull anything across the great chasm; they are already permanent residents of God's Kingdom, and all of its bounty is already in their possession. The atmosphere of their lives is continually saturated in the favour of God, and so the expression of God's love is not measured in individual blessings, but in the unbroken state of the indwelling of the Father's unconditional love.

It is like a divine dare;
dare we entrust our existence entirely into the care of God.

CHAPTER 14

The truth about the kingdoms

For those who attempt to hold dual citizenship, the issues of the natural realm are their primary focus. These issues are real and many, so their ability to hold our focus is strong. As such, our relationship with God is seasoned by the issues of life on earth, and they become the primary element that links us.

The modern church has attempted to counter this imbalance by inserting selfless activities like devotion and worship into the mix, but even these can become self-oriented acts as we engage in them to *feel* God's presence and power.

Jesus Himself said in John 4:23-24, "But a time is coming and has now come when the true worshipers will worship the Father in spirit and in truth, for the Father is seeking such as these to worship Him. God is Spirit, and His worshipers must worship Him in spirit and in truth".

Only as citizens of the realm of the Spirit can we worship God in spirit and in truth. Everything we do as citizens of this world is seasoned by its atmosphere of man-energized virtue…*even worship.* From the noblest to the most base, everything that springs from human effort that is not energized by the Spirit of God is worthless.

These are strong words, so hold on as we get through this bumpy part of the road.

Adam reconstructed our relationship with God such that it depended on the input of both parties. Man performed his religious activities, and in response God provided His presence and protection. These two parties lived in different realms, and the thing that bridged the chasm between them was man-generated religion.

Now that Christ has redeemed us and deconstructed Adam's way, our citizenship in the Kingdom of God has been freely provided to us. We can choose to live there while we finish our days on earth, or we can continue to live as citizens of this world. Of course all Christians are eager to enter into their citizenship in the Kingdom of God and participate in all that it holds, but more often than not we also hold on to the old realm with which we are so familiar.

Even the most noble of all human activities *(worshipping the Most High God of Heaven)*, is tainted by the legacy of Adam if we remain unwilling to step across to His kingdom and entrust ourselves completely into His care.

> **The Kingdom of God operates according to the nature of God; we cannot access it according to the nature of Adam.**

It is also easy to introduce a third dimension into our thinking to accommodate this difficulty as we attempt to resolve the value of human effort.

But there are only two realms – the realm of God, and the realm of darkness. A third realm positioned between the two, from which we step into one or the other, doesn't exist. There are only two realms. While we are here on the earth, we are either citizens of the kingdom of darkness or, if we have received Christ, we are citizens of the Kingdom of Light.

Yet even though we are citizens of the Kingdom of Light, it remains possible for us to continue living according to the law of sin and death. We might possibly do this because we don't trust the Kingdom of God to deliver all that it claims.

The two little girls did this; they didn't trust their new environment to deliver all that it claimed, so they continued living as if they were still a part of their old world – even though they had been delivered from it.

This may seem like madness, yet it is the choice of many.

That's the travesty of religion; it lulls us into a false sense of security in something that is not even real.

The kingdom of this world is actually the kingdom of darkness; they are one and the same place. The only difference is that the kingdom of this world has the natural environment draped over it, which conceals or veils the kingdom of darkness from view.

Similarly the Kingdom of Light is concealed from the view of believers while we remain on the earth; it, too, is veiled by the natural environment.

The amazing thing for believers is that we have been translated from the kingdom of darkness into the Kingdom of Light; we are already citizens of Heaven in exactly the same way as we will be when we die. So the decision to live with a foot in both camps is not such a good idea.

Some people mistake the kingdom of God for the church, and the kingdom of the world for the unchurched. But this is an inaccurate picture of the truth portrayed in the Bible; it is not about denominational affiliation or local community, but invisible spiritual kingdoms. The truth of the matter is that we are in either one or the other – not eventually going there, but already there in real time.

> *As believers we are already citizens of the Kingdom of Light, so it is the height of foolishness if we choose not to live there.*

Okay, let me temper that a bit; foolishness may be a bit strong. It may simply be ignorance. But for those who have grasped the stunning accomplishments of the cross of Christ, it defies reason to remain locked in dependence on the systems of this world.

By the systems of this world, I mean trusting in our own ability to carve out the best life possible, as opposed to leaning back into the unconditional love of God and trusting Him to do it.

At the risk of sounding like a broken record, let me say it one more time: the finished work of Christ in us is astounding in its scope and potential. It surpasses everything we might imagine or hope for as the source of all that we need for life and godliness – yet for lack of spiritual sight and understanding, we relegate it to the category of hopeful speculation. It is not mere Christian speculation that we have been translated to be joint heirs with Christ in the Kingdom of God's extravagant love; it is the most real fact of our new born again existence.

> *We must embrace it for all it is – or not;*
> *there is no middle ground.*

God said that He would rather we be hot or cold, but because we are lukewarm He will spit us out of His mouth – not so much lukewarm in respect to our zeal, but lukewarm in regard to our expectations of the gift of divine life we have received.

The kind of 'hot' that Jesus wants is that we would look Him in the eye and declare, "I believe in all You claim to be, and I surrender my existence into the care of Your love". If we can't do that, then be cold – *but anything in the middle implies that we acknowledge the extravagance of His love gift, but do not wish to entrust our existence into it.*

This is not a popular message; it is unsettling and confronting. It takes great courage to pick ourselves up, look over the chasm between the familiarity of human effort – and the unchartered territory of the Kingdom of Life – and let go of all the props of religion and lifestyle to take possession of the great prize, which is to live in the security of the unconditional love of our Heavenly Father.

Don't get me wrong; this is not a wholesale criticism of Christianity. I face the same day-to-day issues as everyone else, and I also acknowledge that this is very challenging…*but so worth it.*

CHAPTER 15
The veil of this world

When Adam chose to be independent of God by being responsible for his own sense of worth, he effectively lowered a veil between God and us. It was a veil that rendered the spiritual realm and the natural realm as separate environments. The spiritual realm was, and still remains, an environment saturated by God's unconditional love. The natural realm on the other hand became a realm dependant on the performance of humanity to partake in that love.

2 Corinthians 3:14 "But their minds were closed. For to this day the same veil remains at the reading of the old covenant. It has not been lifted, because only in Christ can it be removed".

After Moses met face to face with the Lord, his face was radiant with reflected glory from his time in God's presence, so he covered it with a veil until the radiance faded. This was an Old Covenant phenomenon; it occurred among a people who were under the law. The glory of the spiritual realm was too much for people under the Old Covenant; they had to look away because they were burdened with the condemnation of their sinful condition.

Paul expands on this by explaining that only 'in Christ' can it be removed.

We know that this is theologically true, yet the veil effectively remains in place for many believers because we do not want our minds opened to the truth of God's unconditional love. The Old Covenant is a covenant of legalism; it is conditional on humanity upholding the law – that's what legalism is. It implies that we can lift the veil between God and us by being good.

But it is only 'in Christ' that the veil can be lifted, not 'in our good works'.

For the veil to be lifted from believers they must hide themselves 'in Christ'; from that place 'in Christ' they can gain access to all that is in the

Kingdom of God. If we continue to depend on our behaviour and religious lifestyle to give us access to God's Kingdom, then the veil will remain in place.

For much of my life, I thought that these two were compatible – that I could find my security by hiding myself in Christ and by depending on my good works at the same time. I thought they were linked together, and that God wanted me to present Him with a well-balanced blend. In fact, I thought that was why Christ came, so that He could fix my sin problem so that I could present God with my personal best.

Little did I know that this fundamental misunderstanding kept the veil of the Old Covenant in place. It was like a blind that was always drawn down over the true heart of God, such that I continued to live as if I was subject to the Old Covenant even though I had been translated into the new.

I understand now that God wants me to rest in the work of the cross so completely that I present Him with Christ's personal best, not my own.

In this book I am not attempting to do a thorough treatise on the Old and New Covenants, but it is important to understand the difference between the two and how they relate to us now.

The Old Covenant was a system of laws and commandments that God provided to the children of Israel as clarification of the task Adam had set for them when he chose the Tree of the Knowledge of Good and Evil as his source of life. The Bible is clear that the Old Covenant was faulty and brought death. It was not a reflection of God's heart; God's heart was that we would stop trying to impress Him with our management of good and evil and simply rest in His lavish gift of love. God has nothing invested in the Old Covenant; it was not His idea, nor was it His intent for humanity.

The New Covenant is not a system, it is a person; and His name is Jesus. He abolished the Old Covenant when He nailed it, and all that it represented, to the cross. He was putting an end to humanity's need to manage good and evil as a means to impress God. He was opening up a new way to impress God, faith in the sacrifice of Jesus – the only way humanity can ever partake of the lavish gift of God's love. God has everything invested in the New Covenant – He put up His own Son's life – the highest and dearest of His possessions. It was His idea, and He wants humanity to embrace it with absolute abandon.

The Old Covenant is based on my personal best; the New Covenant is based on Christ's personal best. There is no blending here; if we blend our best with Christ's, then His is diluted. We can only approach God on the basis of perfection…and we get that from Christ.

The veil remains in place for many believers because they have not come to terms with the difference between the covenants; they continue to do religion – instead of being in Christ.

So what exactly is the veil that separates us from God? It is our inability to walk away from the Old Covenant. It is a fear-based way of life that is more worried about pleasing God than resting in His free gift of life. The tragedy is that many well-meaning Christians are still living under a covenant that Christ abolished.

They are more comfortable with Adam's way than Christ's way. Such is the hold that remains on many believers that they are so fearful of getting it wrong *(which is the essence of the Tree of the Knowledge of Good and Evil)*, that they don't abandon themselves to the very reason why Christ came.

I would really like to water this down as I know some will take offence at this, feeling insulted that I seem to be criticising their way of living out the Christian life. But I cannot water down the truth. If I do, it will cease to be the truth. We are saved to partake in the abundance of God's heart… *period!* Anything that follows by way of ministry or service is simply the overflow. The overflow must not be mistaken for the purpose, else we end up back where we started and continue to dine on the wrong tree.

> **The purpose of human existence**
> **is that we might live in the love of God.**
> **That's it!**

Many great ministries have overflowed from that knowledge, and no ministry is of value without it.

There will always be things that the believer would like to see more clearly or gain a greater revelation of. Even after we have abandoned the Old Covenant, we still continue moving toward the light as we renew our thinking. Yet, it is a journey of excitement and discovery, rather than of hopeful longing. The journey is one of unpacking the salvation Jesus gave us and discovering the length and breadth and height of it.

We need the veil out of the way to embark on that journey; it is a type of luggage that is too cumbersome to take on a joy ride with the Holy Spirit. All we need to pack is our confidence in the unconditional love of God. Jesus said that His burden is light, and He was referring to the unconditional love of His Father. It is the lightest load we will ever carry.

The journey of lifting the veil a little bit more each day is the most exhilarating voyage upon which we will ever embark. Day by day, we glimpse more of the wonder of our salvation, and we are overwhelmed little by little by such a stunning love.

It is not a burdensome journey but a thrilling tour of discovery through a landscape we had never before dreamed possible. Discovering the wonder of God's love consumes and overwhelms us. We become so magnetised by this new vista that it becomes our life obsession.

We are like pilgrims with each new horizon of His love for humanity stretching out before us, and as we reach that horizon and view its magnificence, we discover another horizon stretching further again. The term 'immeasurable' comes to mind as we discover that His love for us goes beyond all human comprehension.

CHAPTER 16

Beyond the veil

I would like to tell you that each of us can have a third heaven experience just like Paul…*but I can't say that.* Looking beyond the veil is not a vision we undertake with our natural eyes like when Moses observed the burning bush, or the dream-like trance that Peter had on the rooftop.

From time to time Christians do indeed see visions and experience spiritual visitations, but that is not what I am describing here. I am describing a kind of sight that is always 'on', rather than an exceptional or momentary vision.

It is always 'on' but is generally not perceived by our five senses.

Hebrews 11:1 tells us that faith is "being certain of what we do not see" – it is not a thing that involves our senses, but that does not make it any less real. Just because our eyes can't see the Kingdom of God doesn't make it a figment of our imagination; it simply means that we must choose to view it by faith.

Faith seemed a somewhat nebulous thing for most of my Christian life; it seemed too hard to be confident that I had it right. I had always understood it to be an unshakable confidence that the impossible would happen because of my determination and tenacity. I had seen people try to confess things into existence, or turn on their guts and determination to get God to deliver what they wanted. It was like a Christian conjuring show that required us to get our moves just right or else miss out; but if by chance we got them right, we could somehow create something out of nothing.

But I don't see faith that way anymore.

Faith is no longer about my determination, tenacity, ingenuity or boldness – it is about what I can see with the eyes of my heart.

In other words, there is no point to all the determination, tenacity, ingenuity or boldness if we don't believe we already have what we desire. If we can't already see that it is ours by virtue of the blood of Christ, then forget the religious sideshow and all the conjuring tricks that go with it.

As I said earlier, this sight is always on. We don't need to get in the zone, or press in – it is the atmosphere of our existence. It is like living in a continual open vision of the Kingdom of God.

Jesus did that. Just read the book of John and you will see that Jesus was always in the zone, He lived there – and His earthly body held Him in the natural realm at the same time. Can you hear Him saying, "I only do what I see My Father doing" or "Everything I have learned from My Father I have made known to you"? Jesus didn't need to do anything to be in His Father's presence, and neither do we.

On other occasions Jesus did have a vision or a supernatural visitation, but He was equally conscious of His Father's realm apart from these events. Consider the time when Jesus heard His Father's voice from Heaven in John 12:28-29 and then went on to say, "This voice was for your benefit not mine" – He didn't need a supernatural event because His whole life was a continuous supernatural event.

That continuous supernatural event was that He chose to consider Himself more a citizen of the Kingdom of God than a citizen of the natural world, with the result that the Kingdom of God supernaturally overshadowed His natural circumstances. His natural circumstances pressed in to Him from all sides, but He refused to be distracted by their insistent demands, always believing that they were merely the lesser reality of Adam's fallen world.

> **He was only able to do this
> because He was so secure in a far superior circumstance,
> His Father's love.**

In every other regard He was the same as us and subject to all of the same onslaughts of life; His only difference was that He looked at life on earth through the lens of His Father's love. It was like a filter that changed the nature of earthly circumstances from being an oppressive and crushing offensive, to an impotent and passing event that could not shake His inner contentment.

He chose to be more in His Father's love than in His earthly circumstances, just like He chose to be more in His Father's love than in the boat when the storm came.

This choice would not have been possible for Him had He not been able to clearly see the scale and substance of His Father's love very clearly. It was not a case of 'mind over matter' where He had to convince Himself that something that pressed against Him wasn't real – it wasn't that at all. He actually saw with the eyes of His heart that His Father was greater than any earthly circumstance, and He lived His life 'as if' what He saw was true.

I titled this book 'AS IF' for that reason.

There are two realities that surround us – the kingdom of this world, and the Kingdom of God – and we make the choice to live 'as if' one of them is our primary reality.

I had previously thought that I constructed this new reality out of my determination and boldness, that it was my 'never-say-die' attitude which forced God's hand; but now I see that all I do is simply choose which kingdom will hold me, and I live there in a peaceful confidence.

So the primary thing we must lay hold of *(and the thing which I had the least understanding of)* is that I am secure in my Heavenly Father's love.

This understanding is available to everyone, we don't need to be a leader or have a ministry. This understanding has been distributed equally to everyone – we simply have to choose to make it our own. It is not complicated, so it doesn't require great intellect or theological prowess. That's why even children and those of lowly status can walk with confidence through life – it is available to all.

The only thing that inhibits this understanding is if we mix in our good works as the catalyst that releases it.

When we introduce our natural qualities, they have the effect of minimising the scale and magnificence of the security that is found in our Father's love. Like mixing lemonade with beer, the shandy of human effort may taste sweet, but it has no real substance.

If we want to capture a clear view of our Heavenly Father's love, then we must take a fresh look at the cross of Christ that opened it up to us. The Father's love is a subject that is well established in the public domain of the Christian culture, but it is important that we go beyond the general subject matter and venture to the cross of Christ independently.

My experience is that the subject is so well covered in our Christian dialogues that it has become ordinary – just another item of interest within this great big thing we call Christianity. When that happens, the thing we want most (the reality of God's presence) is lost to us.

I didn't know how to make my personal pilgrimage to the cross of Christ. That subject wasn't in the public domain. So I set out on my journey of discovery to see what it was all about, not knowing if there was anything more there than the well-used rhetoric to which I had become so accustomed.

Even as I write this, there are issues in my life that I would rather weren't there. They are pressing and hard to resolve, so my intention is not to be glib about such a challenging subject. The issues I am speaking of are an offensive against me. They are the result of life dredging up the past and turning it into ammunition to fire at me. I cannot be glib about such matters. And none of us should take our past failings lightly; the ripple effect of the past doesn't disappear just because we become believers.

It can be very heartbreaking to live with the consequences of things we wish we had never experienced or done. Decisions that seemed right at the time can return to condemn us, relationships can be strained or severed, dreams can go up in smoke, hopes and plans can dissolve, and injustices invade. Yet in some form or other, it is the human experience. Those who haven't made any mistakes probably haven't made anything.

That's why a personal pilgrimage to the cross is so important; without it, all we have to work with is our human capabilities that contributed to our problems in the first place.

The cross of Christ resolves the human factor if we will let it.

Our hearts may well remain vulnerable, we might have a tightening across our chest as we face the day's challenges, and sleep may elude us when we need it most. But these physical responses to life's challenges slowly diminish as we learn that the work of the cross can be trusted, and that God has got us.

The cross of Christ is our gateway into another world; it is a world where Jesus is King, and we are hidden in His love and life. This is the world that holds our true identity, and we can live securely in this world by choosing to believe in its claims. These claims are at odds with the pressing circumstances of life. They declare that there can be calm amidst the storm – even as the storms of life buffet us most. And so, if we choose, we can transfer our day-by-day existence across to the safety of this world.

Then, over time, our emotions will fall into line with this greater truth, and true rest will come.

Paul said in Philippians 4:11 that he had "learned the secret of being content" and then followed in verse 13 with his famous statement, "I can do all things through Christ who gives me strength".

It is not our tenacity, determination or even our personal resilience that gives us strength, but the secret of Christ's indwelling that we experience as we learn to rest in Him.

CHAPTER 17
The cross of Christ

In Ephesians 3:3, 4, 9 and 5:32 and again in Colossians 1:26, 27 and 2:2, Paul introduces us to new terminology: he speaks of a 'mystery'. The mystery is 'Christ', and also 'Christ in you'.

This mystery was kept secret by the Old Covenant; effectively the Old Covenant usurped the place held by the indwelling Spirit of God and concealed it from view for the millennia between Adam and Christ. The normal condition of our design as beings inhabited by the Spirit of God became abnormal and hidden in mystery, and in its place was inserted a new normal – the self-made man.

Humanity became a race of the self-managed when we were designed to be Spirit-managed.

The cross of Christ reversed this abnormality and returned us to our true design.

The cross of Christ re-exposed the mystery that had been hidden for ages – Christ in me. It lifted the lid off humanity that had been placed there by Adam's decision to redefine us and gave us back our true nature. The cross was the great reversal; it undid everything that came as a result of the fall and reconnected us to the Tree of Life, which is the only source of everything good.

This is the greatest news that has ever been presented to the human race.

Yet, to a very large degree, we Christians have not laid hold of it. We have accepted Christ's work of substitution for our sins, but we haven't grasped the mystery that was unearthed by that work.

> *We have accepted Christ's message,*
> *but haven't grasped Christ.*

The reason why Jesus took our sins upon Himself was so that we could step back into our original design. That's why He said in John 10:10, "I came that you might have life". He came to give us back the original blueprint that was in God's heart when He first conceived humanity. That original design had human beings living from God's indwelling. God conceived us to be filled with His divine nature as the source of our existence.

Adam remade us to have the self-generating human nature as our source – and Jesus completed the great reversal.

As far as the Father is concerned, He has no capacity to perceive us other than that we are hidden in the life of Christ. From His perspective, we have no independent existence; we are so immersed in Christ that the Father cannot see Adam in us. The nature of Adam has been mysteriously swallowed up.

The Father is of course aware of our earthbound struggles (He knows everything), but He cannot perceive us in them because the work of Christ completely eclipses them from view. As far as the Father is concerned, the original blueprint is now the new us. If He were to perceive us on the basis of Adam's legacy, then He would be elevating the work of Adam to superiority over the work of Christ.

This view that the Father has is akin to a spiritual vision. He is so conscious of the efficacy of the blood of Jesus that He has declared the work of Christ to be our new true identity; it is the vision He has of us. And now, He does not waver from this point of view according to our performance or circumstances. He is fixed to this new view based on the performance of Christ alone. It is a vision that is always on display before the Father – it fills His screen, and the works of Adam are lost in the sea of His forgetfulness.

The cross of Christ has relocated us to the other side of the veil; it is our new habitation.

Our part is to gain the same vision as the Father and see ourselves there too.

This single truth opens the door to the entire Kingdom of God. If we will not come to terms with it, then we will spend the rest of our lives knocking on a door that is already open to us, hoping that God will answer a door that has already been thrown wide open by Jesus. Revelation 3:7 speaks of a door that God has opened that no one can shut – that door is the mystery hidden for ages and now revealed to us in Christ. Jesus has become the new me.

> **The question that remains is this:**
> **"Do I have sufficient confidence in the blood of Christ**
> **to step into my new identity?"**

The two little girls didn't. Their confidence was locked in to their old environment to the extent that they perceived their new environment as nothing more than an improved version of the old. Food was easier to get and shelter was readily available. So their new environment was perceived from the perspective of its ability to provide for their physical needs, when in reality it was so much more than that.

It is this issue that keeps many people knocking at the door, when they should simply walk right in as rightful residents of the place. Adam left us so conscious of our earthly needs that we hardly know how to find refuge in our real area of need – the security of resting in our love union with the Father.

The cross of Christ is primarily not about the resolution of our earthly issues, be it food, restoration, health or any other trouble we may experience here. It is about placing us so securely into the love of our Heavenly Father that these issue pale by comparison and are ultimately resolved as we rest in His goodness.

This 'real' reason why Christ came has eluded many believers for years, effectively robbing us of the best part of our salvation. We are so pressed by the issues of life that they become the platform for our relationship with Him, when a far more wonderful platform for our relationship is available.

Adam left us issue-focussed, and Satan is happy to keep us there – even though we are saved.

The new identity we have in Christ is not primarily issue focussed, it is Father focussed. Not because the issues we face on earth are not real or important, but because the glory of the Father's love is so stunning that it puts them into a new perspective.

So the purpose of the cross was to release us back into the Father's love.

If we relate to the Father only on the basis of our earth-based issues, then we are like the two little girls. They are well fed, clothed and sheltered, but they were made for so much more than that – they were made to love and be loved.

The little girls' parents did not primarily perceive them on the basis of the material needs; they saw them as the objects of their love on whom rested the lavish expression of their hearts.

Our Heavenly Father does not primarily perceive us on the basis of our earthly needs either. In His mind, we are so much more than merely children to be fed, clothed and sheltered; we are the overflow of His being, and as such more precious than any other object in the universe and beyond.

Adam began his days as a love-based being; he revelled in the unconditional love of his Father until that sad day when Satan convinced Him to rebuild his life around himself. From that day on, Adam related to God on the basis of his physical well-being. Everything in Adam's world had physical consequences, and so he lost the ability to revel in the love of God without the addition of human virtue.

Jesus has returned us to a condition that had become just a distant memory for Adam – the ability to let God love us for His own reasons, because He is love.

If the love of God does not blow our minds, then we don't understand what the cross was all about. And until it blows our minds, our response is irrelevant. To perceive Christianity other than through the lens of the unconditional love of God is nothing more than Adam's self-motivation sprinkled with religion.

The best version of a self-motivated man was Adam. We cannot improve on the prototype he developed, so don't think God is standing by hoping we will deliver a better performance than Adam (out of the same bag of tricks). We must stop trying to please God to gain His approval, and rest in the crazy notion that His pleasure is already ours because of Christ.

CHAPTER 18
The doing dilemma

A very long time ago a man named Adam stood before two trees - the Tree of Life and the Tree of the Knowledge of Good and Evil. He had come to a crossroad in his life that could only be resolved by making a choice – this choice was not simply between bad and good, but was actually between two very compelling options.

Sure, temptation by Satan was involved – and some deceitful trickery – but at the end of the day, Adam used his own free will to choose the path humanity would take. He had been warned by God and lied to by Satan; but because of his self-assurance, he preferred the lie to the truth. *After all, it was just a harmless little expedition into the wonderful world of self-fulfilment.*

I wasn't there, so some of this is conjecture, but I imagine that he had no idea what he was getting into – and, by default, what he was getting us into. Suffice to say that it happened, and we humans are now defined by 'what we do' instead of 'who loves us'.

The saddest part is that we have now become so well adjusted to being defined by 'what we do', that we have no idea at all of how to be defined as the objects of the greatest love in existence.

It sounds crazy when you say it like that, but it is nevertheless the normal human condition.

Unravelling all that 'doing' wiring is the tricky part. We want to be defined as the objects of God's love, but we don't know how to fix the part that was broken by Adam. Sure, we understand that Jesus has made us new, but turning off our broken thinking is not so straightforward.

Remember the illustration I used about the two power cables; we can't have the life source from the throne of God flow down those cables if we come as Adam. We must repent, though not of the list of sins we have compiled over a lifetime; it's much bigger than that. We must repent of the nature of Adam. The flow of God's life does not come because we have gone over our list and checked it twice; it comes because we turn our backs on the 'list' mentality that Adam left to us.

If all you have ever done is repent of the individual sins you have committed, then you are probably still stuck in Adam's way of thinking. You are probably still thinking that God will be pleased with you because of your management of good and evil.

You see, when Adam ate from the Tree of the Knowledge of Good and Evil, he effectively became the Tree of the Knowledge of Good and evil; he became a new kind of being who was nourished by his own deeds. We are defined by the thing that gives us life – *you are what you eat*. This is the thing we must repent of. We must repent of the being that Adam made us – all of the self-capacity and self-assurance – and cast ourselves into Jesus.

That is repentance.

We do not repent of sins; we repent of sin. The Bible tells us that Jesus became sin that we might become the righteousness of God, so it follows that before Jesus became sin, we were sin. Sin is not so much a collection of bad deeds and words, but a self-assurance that we can reach God by what we do, or conversely be separated from God by what we do wrong.

Our sins do not separate us from God; it is our choice to be independent of His love as our life source by putting a price tag on it that does that – and the price tag is human virtue.

Notice that the Tree of the 'Knowledge' of Good and Evil is a new kind of knowledge; it is knowing something that was previously not known. That thing is the notion that human virtue (the things we do) is the currency that purchases the presence of God.

> **And that is the thing we must repent of;**
> **that is Adam,**
> **and that is us without Christ.**

Repentance is much more than saying sorry; it is detaching ourselves from our old life source, and in so doing ceasing to be that person. In that regard, we do not need to repent of what we have done, but who we are.

It is much easier to get on our knees at the end of each day and give God an inventory of our failings than it is to look in the mirror and declare to ourselves that the person before us must die. Not the physical death that comes to us all at the end of our days, but the spiritual death of the person who continues the legacy of Adam by allowing their 'doing' to be an obstacle to God's love.

Repentance is having a conversation with the person in the mirror more than having a conversation with God. It is declaring to the person in the mirror that he (or she) is not who he thinks he is – that no matter how much he tries, his life has no inherent worth, and the only way to obtain true worth is to cease to exist as that person.

Then a new person can be born. This new person is made out of the same raw material that God used when He first created Adam. It is a unique design that has not existed on the earth for the ages between Adam and Christ; it is a person who walks around God just by resting in His unconditional love.

This person is full of God without doing anything but letting His love in.

This is not the person in the mirror; that person has died and a new God-man has been born again.

Christ came so that the person in the mirror could die – not to re-invigorate the sons of Adam in their self-made good deeds program.

This is a confronting gospel; on the one hand we are given the Kingdom of God for free, and on the other hand we must give up being the very person we are (the person that has defined our existence up until this point) to lay hold of the reality of it this side of eternity.

This is a very confronting gospel indeed.

CHAPTER 19

The offence of the gospel

As much as I would like to water down the facts, I can't; we simply cannot partake of the Kingdom of God as the offspring of Adam – once we have been born again of God, faith in Christ is our only way forward. It's not that God doesn't want us to bathe in the extravagance of His love, but that if He permits us to mix Christ with Adam, we will do ourselves great harm.

All the way back in the garden in Genesis 3:22-24, God was protecting Adam from himself by keeping him away from the Tree of Life. Had Adam eaten from the Tree of Life as a man who was nurtured by his own ability to manage good and evil, he would have lived for all eternity stuck in the vicious cycle of man-generated virtue – a cycle so terrible that God put an angel with a flashing sword between Adam and the Tree of Life to keep him safe until the redemption of Christ was ready.

God does not lightly keep us from partaking in His life. In fact, Jesus declared in John 10:10 that the very reason He came was to give us God's life – but He will not give us access to His kingdom if we insist on coming with Adam's credentials.

Why? If He were to respond to our insistence on presenting Adam's (man-made) virtue to gain access to His presence, then God would be choosing to allow us to live forever outside of His love. He will not make that which is unconditional to be conditional upon our goodness – *because there is no real love in conditional love.*

He wouldn't allow it with Adam, and He won't accept it from us.

He would rather we played games with religion than to accept our offerings brought in Adam's name. To put it another way, He would rather we came on His terms as the objects of His unconditional love, or not at all.

The gospel of Jesus is offensive because it disqualifies human virtue, and humanity is wired to highly value human virtue.

At this point I will insert my usual disclaimer: this is not about whether we should live good and honourable lives (that is a given), but whether that man-made goodness gives us entrée into the presence of God.

Humanity is accustomed to conditional love; it is the way of the world from childhood to old age –*you must clean your room before you can go outside to play, etc.* There is nothing inherently wrong with conditional love; it has an order and balance to it, but it has no place in the Kingdom of God.

So the gospel of Jesus offends us because it disallows our accepted mode of living as qualification for entry. It is especially offensive to those who have lived their whole lives on the basis of common decency and respect because even these good qualities do not move God; only the shed blood of Jesus moves God.

You might be thinking, "But surely God wants me to be good", and the answer is simple: if the security we find in our good lives causes us to ever second guess our free access to God, then we have valued human virtue too highly. And the flip side is that until we can walk boldly up to the throne of God naked of all human goodness, then any good that we do is still the product of Adam's world.

Are you offended yet?

Perhaps you are offended because I am implying that God doesn't want the person in the mirror – at least, not the person who remains attached to Adam's way of valuing himself.

> **God wants us to value ourselves because of Christ in us, not Adam in us.**

It is hard for us to imagine a life where 'being me' makes sense without all of the things that have contributed to our identity and security thus far, but that is what Jesus is calling us into – a life that is so far removed from the old that it is as if the old person is dead.

We value human qualities too highly because we cannot perceive the staggering contrast between our goodness and God's pure radiant holiness.

Even the most noble, selfless or generous act of human kindness is but a dim glow against the blazing spectacle that is the love of God. So it's not about us stopping doing good things; it's about re-valuing them in the eternal scheme of things.

And it goes even further than that; the best of us, the ones who win Nobel peace prizes and start orphanages, the ones who even give their lives for the sake of the downtrodden, cannot stand before God with a shred of human virtue as their means of opening His arms to them.

Yet if we come to Him naked of our self-worth, He will fill us back up with Himself, just the way He made us to be all those years ago in the garden – and the works of God will overflow from our being like rivers of living water.

That's why baptism is important; it signifies the death of the old self-sufficient person, and the birth of the new God-sufficient person. Baptism implies that I am willing to give offence to my personal best, no matter how good or bad it is, and hide myself in the virtue of Christ. Anything less keeps my old source of security alive.

Imagine walking the halls of Heaven wearing a backpack full of Christ's righteousness and retaining a hand full of your own righteousness. It just doesn't add up – yet that is the instinct that we must overcome. That is the instinct that keeps us from a life carried aloft on the wings of the Spirit.

This stanza from an old hymn – "nothing in my hands I bring, simply to thy cross I cling" – had it right.

And God loves us so much that He will not allow us to follow our instincts. He knows that it is the blood of Christ that releases us from the burden of self-righteousness, and He will not be happy until we are safely hidden there.

So much of modern Christianity directs believers to be the best version of themselves. It shines the light on our potential and urges us to construct a great life from the champion inside us – but this is not the gospel. The true gospel declares to us that we have very little comparative potential, there is no significant virtue, and to build our hope on some *(as yet undiscovered)* ability is like throwing leaves into the wind.

It is imperative that we look away from ourselves to Christ, and it is equally imperative that we do not confuse the innate potential for good inside each of us for the indwelling presence of the Spirit of Jesus.

I told you the gospel was offensive!

CHAPTER 20
Life in the Spirit

Life in the Spirit is the other side of the coin; it is not an addition to Adam's side of the coin.

Life in the Spirit is participation in the life of Christ at the exclusion of all else that might energise us. This is not because God doesn't want us to live big lives or engage in pursuits of all kinds, but because no other source of life can energise us in the same way as the blood of Jesus.

God wants us to have the best.

In the past I would have thought that marrying my human qualities and zeal with Christ's accomplishments on the cross was the plan God had for me. But now I realise that in so doing I am perpetuating the approach of Adam. Jesus didn't come to give a new re-energised legitimacy to the lifestyle of Adam; He came to nail Adam's self-motivation to the cross so that the Spirit could take over the task.

This is perhaps the thing that I least understood about walking in the Spirit, I thought it was a thing that I added to my Christianity, rather than the thing that *is* my Christianity. In other words, I cannot live as a Spirit-energised believer while dipping back in to the world's way of thinking *according to the issue I am facing at the time*.

My old thinking was that some issues are Spirit-resourced issues and some issues are world-resourced issues – but that is wrong!

For the believer, all issues are Spirit-resourced and Spirit-resolved.

God doesn't help those who help themselves – that's not in the Bible.

Remember I mentioned earlier my friend the business man who prays for God's blessing on His business while continuing to cheat on his taxes.

That is a classic example of what I'm talking about: allowing God to resolve the whole of our lives, not just the bits we feel we can't manage on our own.

It may seem expedient to control an aspect of our lives by the world's ways, but in so doing we are turning the blood of Jesus into a thing we use for our convenience, rather than our sole source of supply. The problem is not that cheating on our taxes is a sin (which it is), but that dipping into two kingdoms for our life's supply is effectively declaring that we don't trust the Kingdom of God to live up to the claims it makes.

Can the Kingdom of God provide for our tax problem? Of course it can! But only if we have examined the work of Christ on the cross and determined that it is sufficient for us to put our faith in.

And that is the crux of the problem: we cannot walk in the Spirit without a revelation that the Spirit can be entrusted with every area of our life. And we cannot gain that confidence without a thorough examination of the cross – not a theological examination, but a personal determination that the cross of Jesus is more than an historic event; it is the re-making of us into spiritually alive people.

Spiritually alive people live in the realm of the Spirit.

The realm of the Spirit (the Kingdom of God) contains all that we need for life and godliness (2 Peter 1:3). We do not need to mix in the ways of the world to survive.

So the difference between living from the Tree of Life and the Tree of the Knowledge of Good and Evil is not about choosing between right and wrong, but choosing between faith in God and faith in the world.

Let's unpack this. Adam's actions turned the world into a place that was governed and managed by the code of right and wrong (good and evil). It was an inferior system to the one it replaced, which was governed and managed by the abundance of God's love.

Humanity has lived with Adam's system for so long that it has become the new normal; we instinctively live our lives on the basis of the cause and effect of our actions. We have become so accustomed to controlling our world through the three great world institutions (politics, finance and religion), that we can't imagine an alternative – particularly if the alternative is based in another realm.

So we settle for Adam's inferior model when a dramatically superior system is available to us. Even as Christians we tend to do this, because the visible realm has such a compelling grip on our thinking.

The Christian who wishes to live by the Spirit must overcome this thinking.

Walking in the Spirit is not like walking in the flesh. These two walks operate on an entirely different basis. As such, it is not possible to walk in the Spirit for some of the time and walk in the flesh for the rest of the time.

Walking in the Spirit is not a way of living that we can choose from time to time; it is a place we live in permanently. It is not a lifestyle choice, but the relocation of our thinking to an entirely different realm where everything operates differently. This is the realm for which God originally designed humanity and for which He subsequently re-made us at the cross, and we must choose to relocate our entire existence into it.

The defining truth of this realm is that God can be trusted with our lives, and that His unconditional love is so encompassing that we can cast *every* moment and *every* issue into it.

Trusting God doesn't come easily to the sons of Adam because we are used to selecting the source from which we will draw our supply according to our view of what is expedient at the time. We ask God to help with the big tricky things, and we rely on the world for the smaller mundane things.

I'm not suggesting that we expect God to serve us hand and foot; this is not primarily about receiving from God – but rather that we learn to rest in the environment of His love no matter what is happening in our lives.

Walking in the Spirit has very little to do with getting stuff from God, but everything to do with settling in our minds once and for all that God can be entrusted with our lives.

To get back to the two little girls, they thought they needed stuff; but what they really needed was love. They needed to build a new confidence that they actually belonged in their new home.

We all need God's love, but Adam's world has convinced us we need earthly stuff. However, when we have the love part sorted out, our need for stuff can no longer control or dominate us, because we already have the best. Even important stuff like the well-being of loved ones, justice for the downtrodden, or food for the hungry takes on a new restful perspective when we find our place in God's love.

To illustrate the point, at the time of this writing, Australia has recently been to the polls to elect a new national government. The result of the vote was that Australia chose Scott Morrison to be the nation's Prime Minister. He was previously elected by his peers to be leader of the party, but then the people also elected him for the job. So the following morning, Scott Morrison woke up to the fact that he had been elected to lead one of the great world democracies – what a staggering thing to wake up to.

This morning I also woke up to a staggering fact: I have been purchased by the blood of Jesus to be the dwelling place of the Spirit of the Most High God. The magnitude of this statement cannot be contained in the few words I have employed to write it. My status is even greater than that of the Australian Prime Minister, because the Living God has cast His vote for me and said, "I want you to be my son".

Walking in the Spirit is about realising the magnitude of the fact that I am the recipient of the work of the cross, and that the heart of God has paid the highest price imaginable to reinstate me back into His Kingdom.

This morning I opened my eyes as the child of God.

I can do a lot with this status; all sorts of ministry and service are possible. But none of that is particularly relevant until I grasp the fact that God loves me quite apart from what I do for Him. He loves me so much that He simply longs to have me live as His beloved son.

God wants me.

What an extraordinary thought. The eyes of the greatest being in the universe (and beyond) have been watching me all my life, waiting eagerly for the day when I will let His love in and step into the embrace of sonship.

This is walking in the Spirit.

It is recognizing our citizenship in the Kingdom of God and choosing to live in it.

CHAPTER 21

God wants me

More often than not we think that God wants us to fulfil on earth the mission of the church. Our idea could almost be compared to the wartime poster of Uncle Sam with his pointing finger – God wants *you* for the job at hand.

But I don't think that's accurate.

I don't believe God is primarily concerned about my response, my participation in the Great Commission, or my changed lifestyle – these are simply the overflow of what He really wants, and will appear all on their own… *if I get what He really wants.*

It's easy to get *our* response mixed up with *God's* intentions because of our "cause and effect" mentality. We see the error of our ways and the selfishness that created them and assume God's motivation in savings us is to get us to live in the opposite way, as selfless and giving people.

But what if God's motivation in saving me is not tied up in my reciprocal response but something much higher than that…something that escapes the mind of Adam that we are used to applying to life?

What if God saved me simply because He is love?

Now that would turn my well-constructed theology on its head.

What if God saved me because I am the object of His love and have been for all eternity, and the only way He can be true to Himself is to have me back for His own. What if He invested so much of His nature (the very substance of His being) into Adam, and that His love bond with me is exactly the same as His love bond was with Adam – *His first-ever created child.*

That would mean God wants me because I am a part of Himself; I am the offspring of His love.

A human being produces a child that is the combined physical expression of his parents' characteristics. God produces beings that are the spiritual expression of His greatest characteristic, His loving nature – that's why the gospel of John declares that we have been born of God.

If God wanted me because there was work to do in His kingdom, then my sense of security in God's presence would always be subject to my performance of the tasks He allocated to me. But, no matter how hard I try, I can never fulfil the perfect will of God.

If, on the other hand, God wants me because my relocation back into the kingdom of His love is His perfect will for me, then I can rest secure, because He is the one who fulfils His perfect will, not me.

This is such an elusive truth for the mind of Adam – a mind that cannot conceive human worth other than through the actions it produces. But we have the mind of Christ – a mind which values human worth in a completely different and superior way. I am of value because the nature of God is such that God is obsessed with loving me.

God is obsessed with me.

It sounds a tad heretical until you think about it. "God so loved the world" is a phrase we use all the time, but we generally don't take it to the divine and eternal lengths that the true character of God implies. God is not restrained like humans; He is full on, and He doesn't measure His response like we do. When He loves, He loves with His whole being; and when He wants someone, He wants that person with His whole being.

And He wants me *(and you)*...

Adam's mind balks at this. How could God possibly want me so much when I have no inherent worth – nothing to warrant such extravagance, nothing to attract such obsessive behaviour?

That's the problem with the thinking that Adam handed down to us; it has no capacity to view the true heartbeat of God because it always applies the filter of human performance.

The thinking of Adam keeps us on the treadmill of picking petals from daisies – He loves me, He loves me not, He loves me, He loves me not – all dependent on how well I am doing at the time.

But try to imagine living without that filter. Try to imagine a life where the flood of God's obsessive love is not restricted by my performance on the stage of life on earth, where it is free to fill every nook and cranny of my being because the dam wall of human behaviour that holds it back has been broken down. That would be really living, no longer wondering if everything is okay between God and me, but simply living in the assurance that the filter Adam applied to God's love has been removed at the cross.

Now, I don't want you feeling nervous that I am advocating a life of irresponsibility; quite the contrary is true. This is the only way that we can actually live a life that is pleasing to God. The indwelling Spirit of God is so much better at producing goodness in us than the Tree of the Knowledge of Good and Evil.

But it takes place in a way that is quite foreign to Adam's way.

Goodness is not something we do; it is something we are.

In Adam's case, once he stepped out of his union with God, goodness was something he had to self-generate by producing good deeds, words and thoughts. But when we rest in the union with God that was restored to us at the cross, goodness is automatically transferred to us like a blood transfusion from God's own heart – we don't do anything except receive it.

> *We were made for this flow of life;*
> *it is our true design and purpose.*

But our old way of thinking is not satisfied with this; it cannot comprehend that there is a goodness that can be received which requires no human input at all. We have become so familiar with man-motivated goodness that is the result of human effort that we cannot imagine that a person can truly be good without playing the part.

We have become masters at manoeuvring our theology to reflect our internal belief system (which is based on Adam's thinking), that we can't embrace anything new or different.

And the newest and best thing of all is that God wants me.

He doesn't want me in an altruistic or charitable sense; He wants me in a passionate, obsessive sense. This is not God taking the high moral ground and deciding to rescue us because no one else can; this is God compelled by the insatiable love urge that is in Him, giving up all that is precious to Him to buy us back – because He simply cannot be without us.

It doesn't sound like the God I grew up with, who was more of a remote observer than a deeply passionate lover of humanity. I have had to make some big adjustments in my thinking to get to this place. Some of Adam's ideas didn't go away easily. But now that I can see it, it is so obvious; God wants me because of who He is.

CHAPTER 22
But do I want God

That is the million-dollar question. Of course I want God…but do I want God to be Himself?

Or to put it another way, do I want God as long as He fits in with my expectations of who He should be? Expectations, I might add, that I picked up from Adam.

I came into this whole Christian thing with a need; we all did. It was a need based on my experience thus far in Adam's world – the need to fit in somewhere. I couldn't articulate this need so clearly at the time; I just did whatever was natural to me, whatever expression suited my personality, and took my place in the great big Christian community.

It is sometimes said that people join churches for many different reasons, but they stay because of community – they have found where they fit, a place they can call home. And that was me. I found myself fitting into a community that believed in God. And if that fit didn't work out after some time, then I moved sideways into another community where I seemed to fit again.

God seemed to fit into that community, too. We were all there together: me, God, and all the rest of the church, all getting along and doing the stuff that believers do. Some seemed to be more connected to God and some not so much, but it didn't matter because we had all decided to be connected to each other.

So this arrangement generally worked out okay for me, but now I'm not so sure it was working for God.

When Adam took leave of God's presence, he had a fellowship void. It was a God-shaped void, so Adam went about solving this problem by filling this void with the next best thing…*people*.

Adam was designed by God to be in continuous, intimate union with his Heavenly Father, and then to express the joy of this union into the natural realm by loving it and the people in it. But Adam swapped this around; he constructed a new kind of union between himself and the created world, including the people in it, and then from time to time he turned towards God and offered up a man-made form of love called religion.

So I found myself being like Adam and thinking that was the way it was supposed to be.

I found myself attempting to find God as the overflow of my place in Christian community.

By now you probably know where I am heading with this: I had repositioned God into overflow status. I had given Him the role of turning up from time to time depending on the religious activity that was happening. The Christian community became the diverse distribution centre of myriad activities, and occasionally they even pulled God out of their bag of tricks.

I had this all mixed up. I was living in Adam's swap, and I didn't even know it.

And what's more, I expected God to be that kind of God.

So in reality my answer to the question "But do I want God?" was no! Not unless He was prepared to be what I had decided He should be.

Now, I must add another disclaimer: None of this was deliberate. I didn't set about re-making God in my own image; it was just natural for me to think this way and perceive God through the filter of my Adamic mindset. I had no way to think differently because my entire experience up until that time was based upon the workings of a realm that didn't understand God.

I was like the two little girls. I had been transported into Nirvana, but I didn't have any experiences I could call upon to show me how to live there. And I had never been exposed to a love without strings attached before, a love which was from a different realm – where unconditional love is the binding factor, not human virtue.

I expected God to be like me.

It has been both a relief and a delight to discover that He isn't. Over the last ten or so years, I have slowly been unpacking the God that Jesus knew, and He barely resembles my old God at all. At last the whole thing is starting to make sense. I am falling back into the un-swapped union for which I was made, and it's so much better.

I do want God.

And at long last, I want Him to be true to Himself too.

So a new adventure began for me. I set out to discover who God was. These were uncharted waters. Nobody seemed to understand what I was going on about or why this was even necessary – so I set off alone. Like the navigators of old, I set off to see if there was something more out there beyond the horizons of my familiar environment…and I discovered a new world order.

> *God was different in this new world.*
> *He seemed to be able to be something*
> *that He couldn't be in my old world –*
> *He could be Himself.*

When I first stepped ashore into this new realm, I expected it to be more or less the same as the environment I was used to, albeit perhaps a little more untamed. I thought God was the same everywhere, and it was just a matter of making some fine adjustments so that I could fit in here, just as I had done from time to time to fit into any new church environment.

But strangely, nothing seemed to work like it used to anymore. I tried to stuff God back into the box I had built for Him over a lifetime of religious involvement, but He wouldn't go in – and finally I realized that He was a completely different person in His own home.

And then began the real adventure – the discovery of who God was, and who I am as a result.

This journey of discovery had two parts. Just as the two girls had to embark on a long journey to a land that was altogether foreign, so did I. That was the part about discovering who God was, and it was like leaving behind all that I knew so that I could have fresh eyes to see God.

And the second part was learning to be a resident of this brave new world – it was the re-discovery of the true me.

CHAPTER 23

The true God

In my opinion, the greatest failing of modern Christianity is that we have painted God in a way that is quite untrue to His real character.

Religion has accused our Heavenly Father of something of which He is not guilty – judging us according to our management of good and evil. We should actually level this accusation against our earthly father, Adam; he is the one who chose this method for determining our worth, not God.

Ever since Adam chose the Tree of the Knowledge of Good and Evil as the diet for humanity's spiritual nourishment, we have perceived the character of God through the broken thinking that came with it.

This doesn't end when we are saved, but it does position us to deal with it by renewing our minds.

There is a hangover from our pre-saved minds that continues to mix the old and the new, the old judgemental God with the new loving God.

We think Jesus saved us so that we can finally live good lives that God will judge as acceptable.

We rightly consider God's holiness as absolute and without flaw, but then deduce that the ultimate expression of that holiness is judgement against all unholiness. While it is true that Adam's actions created a new world order – *'I want to be judged by how well I am doing'* – it is no longer true of us.

This residual attachment to valuing human virtue is founded on the notion that God created us with a mandate to replicate His character – that God made humanity to do good and to avoid doing evil.

And that's where we have been wrong.

God's means of providing us with the necessary compatibility with His holiness that would enable us to stand in His presence is so superior to man-centric virtue that it makes that system look like kindergarten.

Such statements as "the Ten Commandments are a reflection of God's heart" are a complete misunderstanding of the character of God. That kind of thinking implies that God has an expectation of humanity that we will please Him by living wisely and well, and that the Ten Commandments provide a useful guideline to do this.

But nothing could be further from the truth; adherence to any code of behaviour is absolutely incompatible with the holiness of God. It implies that we have within us an innate capacity to live good lives for God – and worse still, that God wants this from us.

This thinking is at home with Adam's way, but completely out of step with the Spirit.

The superior way is to have our eyes fixed on Jesus.

Adam would have us fix our eyes on Jesus so we can replicate His behaviour and produce an improved kind of virtue that is modelled on Jesus' life.

But the Spirit operates in a completely different way to this. The Spirit wants us to fix our eyes on Jesus so that *He* can be the author and perfector of our faith – *not us*.

This characteristic of God (that He does it all) has been muddied by my hangover insecurity – that God is watching me to see if I will live right. The two are completely incompatible, and they have caused modern Christianity to paint a false picture of God.

So we must deal with this problem if we are to discover the true character of God.

All of the commentary so far in this chapter is a preamble to what I really want to say. It explains the problem, but now I want to swing our attention across to the truth and bring into focus the facts about God that we have been missing.

The nature of God possesses an extravagance that is diminished by Adam's way of thinking. This extravagance is so scandalous that we well-meaning Christians have retreated from it for fear of excluding some not-negotiable fact that we can't quite pin down. In other words, we are so scared of getting it wrong, that we don't get it right.

It takes a certain amount of courage to embrace a new truth to the point where it becomes our life-defining fact.

Extravagance is not a word that I immediately thought of in regard to the character of God; I was more likely to drift towards benevolence or tolerance, but certainly not extravagance. In so doing, I was holding God in Adam's world and not allowing God to be who He really is when He is at home.

We are all a bit like that; the environment in which we find ourselves very often determines how we express our true selves – and the environment Adam (and I as well) fabricated for God has limited His expression to my expectations of Him.

So I must learn to be comfortable with an extravagant God.

The only way for me to make that shift in my thinking is to make a shift in my residency; I must relocate myself to God's place and move in with Him. This relocation is not to be at all tentative. It is necessary that I consider myself to be a bona fide resident of the Kingdom of God and not simply an unworthy guest.

Only extravagance can make that happen.

Paul makes quite an issue of the scale and nature of God's love for us in his prayer for the saints found in Ephesians 3:14-21. He labours the point, hammering home how important it is that we be rooted and established in the love of Christ – a love that even surpasses knowledge and fills us with the fullness of God, an immeasurable, beyond imagination kind of love.

It's time to slow things down and spend a little time absorbing this.

It's time to do some recalibrating. Could this possibly be describing me – me with the train wreck of a life, me who defaults to accepting the theory about God without daring to embrace His extravagant love as my own?

What a crazy paradox: when we diminish ourselves out of our misguided humility, we actually diminish God too. We would never deliberately give offence to God by reducing His greatness just to get Him to fit in with our human insecurities, but that is exactly what we do when we shy away from accepting His extravagance.

How extravagant is God? Beyond anything we can imagine, even surpassing our wildest estimations, His extravagant heart is so far beyond the capacity of our finite minds to grasp that we don't even touch the scale of it. We cannot exaggerate God.

How does one recalibrate someone that is so far beyond calibration, someone that is so 'off the scale'?

Actually, it's impossible. All we can do is recalibrate ourselves.

CHAPTER 24
The true me

The trick is to stop thinking of myself as the sum of my human characteristics, my past successes and failures, and so on, and dare to ask God what He thinks of me.

Because the fact is, whatever God considers to be the truth about me is the truth, and everything else is just static. And there is a lot of static, a lot of background noise that tries to block out the truth about me.

When the two little girls came to Australia, they brought with them the background noise of the past. This background noise was entirely true. It wasn't merely a fabrication of their impoverishment; but the moment they crossed over into Australia, it ceased to be the truth for them.

The same can be said of us. The background noise of our past, that time before we crossed over into trusting in Jesus, was also very real. There is no denying it. But now, it has ceased to be the truth about us.

How can that be? You might wonder how someone's history can cease to define them. That history happened, and there is no denying it; so how can it stop being relevant when it continues to exert its influence on our circumstances? We can't just pretend it never happened, like burying our heads in the sand and hoping it will go away.

> *Yet God doesn't see us in our circumstances;*
> *He sees us in Christ.*

This is not just another clever line that I have come up with to get you to arrive at my preferred destination. This is an eternal fact: we are already in that destination, the Kingdom of God.

The problem for many of us is that we have not actually processed this truth. We have been swept along by the great big 'doing' machine of

Christianity, thinking that's all there was, when a far superior truth has come into our lives. We have been translated to another place that doesn't work the same way.

But to live there, we must go back to the beginning and process the truth about Jesus.

It's a bit scary to think that you might have been a Christian for your whole life (or even just a few weeks) and haven't yet processed Jesus. It's like we leapfrog over Jesus and get straight into the activities of Christianity, just like the little girls leapfrogged their new parents' love and got on with shoring up their circumstances.

So if we want to truly take ownership of the truth that God sees, we must deal with Jesus once and for all. We must get inside His skin and find out from Him what it was all about.

If you don't want to do that, then close this book right now. There is no point in continuing.

If all you want is to have your circumstances resolved, but don't actually want to discover the truth about Jesus and embrace that truth as the new fact that defines you, then put this book in the bin quickly – because your life may very well be turned upside down if you continue reading.

I'm not talking about becoming a religious fanatic; but I am talking about discovering something so scandalous that you can no longer be the person you were. This reality will change you.

You will be presented with a new take on your circumstances, one that steps around the great big machine called Christianity; and then you will need to decide if you can put your trust in it. This decision is made more difficult by the fact that you have probably attempted this before, yet in the past you tried to do it by pulling Jesus into the great big machine with you and asking Him to be your passenger.

Now you are stepping into His mode of transport (the Holy Spirit) and trusting Him to steer you out of your impoverishment and into a new kind of life.

When Jesus saved us, He drew a line through our past. As far as God is concerned, we have lived two lives: one as a person who lived from the resources of the kingdom of this world, and one as a person who lives from the resources of the Kingdom of God.

The first thing we discover when we begin to process Jesus is that, although we have been made citizens of the Kingdom of God, we have continued to live from the resources of this world.

That must stop.

We must step over the line and entrust ourselves to Jesus even though our circumstances and our past experiences scream out "don't do it".

And I agree that if we can't clearly see the work that Jesus accomplished in us at the cross, then we are better off sticking with the resources of our old lives. Otherwise we are trying to pull Jesus into our impoverishment and asking Him to wave His magic wand a second time.

He did that once and for all at the cross. He entered our impoverishment and dealt with its hold over us – and now we partake in all He accomplished by entrusting our lives into His care.

So what exactly happened when Jesus entered our impoverishment?

What did He accomplish when He was down here that changes who we are now?

We became the objects of God's extravagance again, just like Adam was before he decided to head off and fend for himself. Jesus has returned us to our pre-sin condition, and now it's all about living as the objects of God's extravagant, unconditional love.

It overflows into our earthly circumstances, and it also overflows into the things of our past that have stayed with us in spite of our best efforts to rid ourselves of them. But it's not primarily about those things; it is about learning to live in the joy and wonder of Heaven early, even before we leave this life when we die.

In other words, it's about stepping into a different kind of joy, one that is not found in or controlled by the kingdom of this world. It's the joy that is normal in Heaven. It is the joy Jesus knows and lives in everyday; it is a joy that comes from discovering (deeply and personally) that I am safely hidden in God's extravagant love.

For fear of sounding like a cracked record again, let me say one more time, don't measure the reality of this joy by whether your circumstances are in order. Measure it by the extravagant act of love that was expressed to us at the cross.

You might be thinking that the extravagance expressed at the cross is too intangible, that your needs are far more 'present tense' and beyond the reach of an event that happened in the Middle East two thousand years ago. But you would be wrong. That event has a unique eternal capacity to span the ages as if it were occurring in real time today.

That is the reason why we must get up close and personal with the cross of Jesus. It is the only event in human history which is truly eternal. It is not limited by the passage of time; in fact, it translates our time-based lives into the eternal realm where the extravagant love of God is on tap all day long.

The true me is eternal.

The cross of Jesus did that; it took me from the realm of time and translated me into eternity. Now I live in the same place Jesus does, and the extravagant love of God is the air I breathe.

The air you breathe? I hear you say...that's a stretch!

Ok, a bit of poetic licence there, but I'm trying to make a point that is so far beyond our imagination that I had to get your attention somehow – otherwise, we may all just settle for the status quo and be no better off.

I lived too much of my life reading over certain Scriptures that made astonishing claims as if they weren't there. I did it because they didn't line up with the evidence on the ground – so nothing really changed for me except my use of all the familiar Christian rhetoric.

So, one of these must be true: either the extravagant, unconditional love of God, or the contrary evidence on the ground.

Take your pick.

For most of my life, I picked the more conservative option, but continued with the faith talk just in case anyone was watching. So in the final analysis, I chose my beliefs based on the evidence in the natural realm, instead of the Word of God from the Spiritual realm.

I don't do that anymore. I am not perfect at trusting God, but I have stepped over the line and determined that I will think, and live, as a citizen of the Kingdom of God. I don't want to have to explain to God when I see Him face to face at the end of my earthly life why I didn't live in the extravagance of His love, but instead chose the impoverishment of depending upon the ways of the world.

I want to live in eternity early.

So here's the thing: the extravagant nature of God is a given. It has been fully and powerfully demonstrated at the cross. *It's in the public domain.* I can either live out my days on planet earth as if it's true, or not. God can't force me to take my place around the great banquet table of His love. Only I can do that.

> ***Only I can decide that the sacrifice of Jesus was enough for me.***

Only I can make the choice to stop doing religion to get God's attention and take Him at His word. My place at His table has been paid for…*when will I take my seat?*

It occurred to me some time ago that I had spent a significant part of my life making statements about faith, but not actually living my life as if they were true. That's why I gave this book the title 'As If' – because I wondered how different my life would look if I lived *as if* everything I claimed to believe about God were actually true.

So I decided to wipe the slate clean and rewrote my faith statement. I decided that no Christian cliché or well-used Christian catch phrase would pass my lips unless I really believed it and was ready to live *as if* it was true and stake my life on it.

For a little while, there wasn't much on the list. If it didn't pass the 'As If' test, then it didn't make the cut. Only statements that I was ready to be truly defined by were added. My Christianity would be a bond between God and me now, not between me and the culture that seems to thrive on cheap talk. I had to be able to look Jesus in the eye and tell Him that I entrusted my whole existence into His integrity…before any pious Christianese would pass my lips.

For a while, it seemed like I was going backwards. I just could not pretend, so more often than not, I said nothing.

But ever so slowly, I have rediscovered what I believe – except now, it's real.

CHAPTER 25
As if

The first thing to change was my thinking about the presence of God. The Bible declares that God will never leave me nor forsake me; it talks about the ever-presence of God so much that I decided to stop reading over it and put it on my list. From that moment forward, I decided to live *as if* God *was* with me – intimately and eternally present in me and every circumstance I face.

For a little while, I found myself pulled in two directions. I was so used to asking God into my circumstances that I did it instinctively, and I was so used to singing songs about 'coming into God's presence' that the words came out of my mouth before I had time to decide if that was how it really was. But slowly I am bringing my language into agreement with the truth; God is continually present with me because Jesus has translated me into the Kingdom where He lives.

Then came my prayer life. I had lived my life in such a comfortable awareness of my earthly circumstances that I had no idea how to pray *as if* I was a person who had been transformed by the greatest of all circumstances in human history – the cross of Christ. I had prayed towards an external God, instead of the reality of the mystery hidden for ages – God in me.

So I found myself dumbstruck whenever I decided to pray. I had to learn how to have a continual conversation with God, instead of one that involved re-qualifying myself to be in His presence every time I decided to talk to Him. It has meant that I have had to stop thinking of God *as if* He is a human being who requires the proper introduction before we get down to business, because the introduction was made once and for all by Jesus when He brokered my reunion with God on the cross.

So now I just talk to God. It's not fancy and it's not pious; it's just a conversation between intimates.

My day-to-day conversations also underwent change. I found myself up against a roadblock whenever I attempted to make a statement that I didn't personally own. I couldn't form the words as easily as I used to. It had become quite foolish to say something just because it was a part of the common language of Christianity when it contradicted my 'As If' rule. So I don't talk much like a Christian anymore, even when I am with other Christians – I just try to talk *as if* everything I say would come out of my mouth if Jesus were in the room…*which He is.*

I don't confess my sins anymore either; the Bible tells me that God has forgotten them before I even committed them, so I don't bring them up. I figure that God has a better grasp of the truth than I do, so I just approach Him *as if* I had never sinned at all. If I were to do otherwise, then I would be living *as if* the sacrifice of Jesus had not accomplished what it claims, and that my sins remain simmering under the covering of God's grace, when in reality there is no sin in Heaven (even my awful sins), and Heaven is my new home.

But the biggest 'As If' of all has been that I have decided to live *as if* I am the object of the greatest love in the universe. The apostle John did it first. He coined the term "the disciple whom Jesus loved" to describe himself, even though we know Jesus loved them all equally. John simply decided to live his life *as if* the love of Jesus was in and through every moment of his life – he decided to lay claim to the most extravagant fact in all eternity, that he was the one God loved.

I must confess that my past instincts have fought against this; it's not natural for me to elevate myself to such a lofty status. But in resisting, I have minimised the work of the cross. I have held it in my doctrinal folder instead of shifting it across to my 'As If' folder. The work of the cross is no use to me in my doctrinal folder; it either redefines me in every way… *or why even bother?*

So the greatest battle I wage is against myself as I try to be true to the life of Christ that lives in me.

I have had a lot of conversations with myself these past few years. At times it seems like I am trying to teach an old dog new tricks; but, in spite of that, a strange and wonderful thing has slowly begun to take place. I am beginning to live *as if* all that I believe is actually true.

I am discovering that I am what I believe.

It's not that I have to believe it into existence, but rather that it is an eternal fact that cannot be manifested in my life until I believe it to be true.

Previously I subconsciously manifested other things into my life, things that were related to the evidence on the ground, things that were supported by the natural information about my life and me.

But now I stop and have a little talk with myself. I take inventory of the eternal facts, not the natural ones – and I live *as if* the eternal ones are the primary truth about me.

I haven't perfected this yet; I probably never will, but that's not the point. The point is that I have decided to step over the line. From now on my identity is hidden in Christ, not in my own personal best (or worst). I have decided to see myself like God does.

What does that look like in real terms?

It looks like a decision – a decision that is internal. It is not primarily about any external expression or action. It is a decision to change my mind about myself and begin living my life as if all I believe about God is actually true.

It is not like a resolution, which requires an action to validate it. This is just a decision between me and myself. I don't have to convince anyone else that this decision is real, but I cannot fool myself.

It's not even a decision between God and me. He is already completely happy with me as He sees me hidden in the sacrifice of Christ. But He does offer me an opportunity to *live* as a changed being – one who is not only changed eternally, but one who also chooses to grasp that eternal change and be redefined by it in real time.

There was a time when I thought that the highest and noblest expression of my Christianity was to submit myself to God's will, to repent of my old life and choose to serve God in any way, and in any place, He might choose.

But now I realise that it is far higher and nobler that I surrender myself to His love, that I repent of my old life of trying to please God by what I do and choose to live my life as the object of His unconditional love.

> *These are two entirely different scenarios.*
> *The first is defined by my life given to God;*
> *the second is defined by God's life given to me.*

This is at the heart of the decision I have made. I have decided to hide myself in God's love. I have decided to cross over the chasm of my impoverished thinking and simply, yet completely, entrust my life to Him.

Don't worry, I'm not abandoning a life of service; but I am elevating the love of God so far above my response that it makes my service pale into insignificance.

This is where the modern church has had it all mixed up. We have been taught and exhorted, preached at and trained, to think that God is obsessed with getting us motivated to serve Him and each other – that the godliest thing I can do with the message of salvation is to respond in kind and live a life worthy of Him.

And we carry that thinking over into the circumstances of life and think that God can't respond to us unless we are doing all the Christian stuff we can think up.

But we don't need motivational preaching; we need to discover Christ for ourselves – because then we are transformed from the inside.

Far too many Christians are sitting in the pews each Sunday who have never discovered Jesus for themselves. They have been so busy doing church that they haven't slowed it all down, looked into the eyes of the lover of their souls and drunk deeply of the wonder and joy they find there.

This is the purpose of our salvation, and until we make this discovery, our lives of frantic activity are nothing more than an extension of Adam's mad experiment into self-realization.

A day is coming when those who sit in the pews will hear about the love of Jesus with no strings attached. They will drink deep draughts of the unconditional love of God and be so transformed by it that the world will sit up and notice.

And we will again become a church who is obsessed with Jesus. We will be like Paul who declared that he considered everything else to be rubbish compared to the surpassing greatness of knowing Christ Jesus his Lord.

The day is coming when we will decide that the Holy Spirit can be trusted to do the motivating, and all we need to do is fix our eyes on Jesus, the author and perfector of our faith.

So that's what I've decided to do, to look Jesus in the eye and live my life *as if* His love for me is enough to carry me through everything.

It's simple really.

So simple that anyone can do it, and I don't know how I could have missed it for so long.

Conclusion

The crucifixion of Jesus is an event that occurred about two thousand years ago on a hill outside Jerusalem. It is the most significant event in human history; it even defines our calendar and sets our history within the context of BC and AD. Yet it is so much more than a milestone event along the passing parade of human history – *it ended human history.*

For many people the end of human history is delayed until the day when they die and step out of history and into eternity. But for some people, they choose to enter eternity early.

The crucifixion of Jesus is different than every other event that has occurred on our planet because it bridges the chasm between time and eternity – it has the capacity to convey us from the kingdom of this world into the Kingdom of God.

As soon as Jesus rose from the dead, the crucifixion became an event that was eternal; it couldn't be contained in the realm of time any more than Jesus could. And now, that eternal event hovers and broods over us all, it is no longer held in place by a moment in time, but is now present tense over all of human history.

And so it stands before each of us, challenging us to either fully accept and embrace the claims it makes, or reject it out of hand.

But there is no middle ground; it is not that sort of thing. It is not like joining a club that provides us with activities and benefits that we come and go from as our lives change; it is the end of our history and the beginning of our eternity.

The cross of Jesus is present tense and hovers before each one of us. It calls each one of us to make a decision about its validity. Will we entrust ourselves to it or will we continue to depend on our own ability to manage things…*and ask God to help when things get a bit too hard?*

If we dare to entrust ourselves to Him, everything changes.

We find that the existence we once knew is crucified with Jesus, and that we are resurrected with Him into new life. This new life takes place in another realm known as the Kingdom of God; it is our new home even though we also remain for a little while longer in the natural realm on planet earth.

Those who entrust themselves to the cross of Jesus have become eternal beings in every regard, and when they die they will be no more citizens of Heaven than they already are; they crossed over from death to life long before they died.

They decided to look Jesus in the eye in the same way that the apostle John looked Jesus in the eye as He hung on the cross 2000 years ago; it was just as real as if they were there in person. They decided to entrust themselves to a present tense love and make the great crossing.

Sure, the issues of life continue to rage all around, just as they will continue to apply their havoc against the lives of all who live on planet earth – but they have lost their sting for us because the glory of God is now our environment, and we are safely seated around the banquet table of His great love.

Drink deeply.

Cheers,

Graeme

www.ingramcontent.com/pod-product-compliance
Lightning Source LLC
Chambersburg PA
CBHW072059290426
44110CB00014B/1751